Working toward an Equitable and Prosperous Future for All

Praise for *Working toward an Equitable and Prosperous Future for All: How Community Colleges and Immigrants Are Changing America*

"Members of the Community College Consortium for Immigrant Education have provided a significant set of resources with the publication of the companion books, *Working Together: How Community Colleges and Their Partners Help Immigrants Succeed* and *Working toward an Equitable and Prosperous Future for All: How Community Colleges and Immigrants Are Changing America.* Community colleges are the natural choice for immigrants to learn the skills needed to adapt to a new environment and to become successful contributors to American society and our economy. These companion books, written by experienced community college leaders, provide valuable information to assist our colleges to develop and strengthen programs for this important group of students."—**George R. Boggs, PhD, superintendent and president emeritus, Palomar College; president and CEO emeritus, American Association of Community Colleges; and chair, Phi Theta Kappa board of directors**

"These books offer deep insight into the most promising, innovative models for addressing barriers to economic opportunity for immigrants and English language learners and understanding how partnerships can help strengthen, sustain, and replicate this work. You could spend the next few years traveling across the country to meet these thought leaders and see their programs in action. Or you can acquire the knowledge from the frontlines in this two-book compendium."—**Peter Gonzales, president and CEO, Welcoming Center for New Pennsylvanians**

"This publication highlights effective community college partnerships, policies, and programs that support immigrant and refugee students. Community colleges across the country act as a bridge to the middle class and careers with economic mobility. Community college leaders committed to equitable student success can benefit greatly from the promising practices shared by many CCCIE members, including the chapter on the Oregon Career Pathways framework."—**Mark Mitsui, president, Portland Community College**

"A book with solutions! As community college practitioners, we must quickly create workforce solutions for emerging career opportunities for diverse industries and diverse communities. *Working toward an Equitable and Prosperous Future for All: How Community Colleges and Immigrants Are Changing America* provides us with many solutions to meeting the current and future workforce challenges of our immigrant communities."—**Girard Melancon, vice chancellor, Workforce Education, Baton Rouge Community College**

"The authors have further informed the consciousness of each reader by providing an applicable strategy. Community college leaders now have an additional roadmap to borrow from when they begin, create, or enhance their institutional approaches to deeper inclusive practices. This text goes beyond the aspirational and achieves tangible proven practices. These are discussions and questions necessary for all our communities to create a platform for current and future leaders to spring forth."—**Michael Torrence, president, Motlow State Community College**

"In the 21st-century global knowledge economy, the only ticket to a middle class and a prosperous life is a post-secondary degree. At community and state colleges across the country, innovative and trend-setting initiatives and partnerships are full force ahead to ensure all individuals succeed, especially those who are new to our country. This book highlights the unique role these partnerships play in the growth and development of our communities, so everyone has access to an equitable and prosperous future."—**Eduardo J. Padrón, president, Miami Dade College**

Working toward an Equitable and Prosperous Future for All

How Community Colleges and Immigrants Are Changing America

Edited by Jill Casner-Lotto
with Teresita B. Wisell

ROWMAN & LITTLEFIELD
Lanham • Boulder • New York • London

Published by Rowman & Littlefield
An imprint of The Rowman & Littlefield Publishing Group, Inc.
4501 Forbes Boulevard, Suite 200, Lanham, Maryland 20706
www.rowman.com

6 Tinworth Street, London SE11 5AL

British Library Cataloguing in Publication Information Available

Library of Congress Cataloging-in-Publication Data Available

ISBN: 978-1-4758-5253-0 (cloth : alk. paper)
ISBN: 978-1-4758-5254-7 (pbk. : alk. paper)
ISBN: 978-1-4758-5255-4 (electronic)

∞ ™ The paper used in this publication meets the minimum requirements of American National Standard for Information Sciences Permanence of Paper for Printed Library Materials, ANSI/NISO Z39.48-1992.

Cover image: *We Are All Immigrants*, 30" × 30", mixed media, 2005, by Huong—an immigrant, mother, and war refugee working tirelessly for decades for peace education through art. *We Are All Immigrants* is part of the Huong Peace Mural, which was more than 20 years in the making; it depicts 30 years of searing memories that bring history to life and portrays the universal pain of war and hope for peace.

Contents

Foreword

Our society has undergone dramatic changes with the increase in the immigrant population—a transformation that brings both challenges and opportunities. Ensuring effective education for all students reflects the core mission of community colleges: to respond to the changing needs of our communities and provide open and meaningful access to all students.

Although community colleges have always been recognized for serving diverse populations and consider diversity a core shared value, many are going even further by adopting diversity, equity, and inclusion plans; hiring diversity and inclusion officers; embedding diversity and inclusion in the college's policies; and encouraging an on-campus culture focused on diversity (Ashley A. Smith, "Focus on Diversity at Community Colleges," *Inside Higher Ed*, April 13, 2018, accessed September 18, 2018, https://www.insidehighered.com/news/2018/04/13/growing-number-community-colleges-focus-diversity-and-inclusion). Incorporating diversity and inclusion in an academic environment means more than just considering race. Understanding diversity is the ability to listen effectively to and develop an understanding for different cultures, ideas, backgrounds, and abilities. Managing the convergence of these different factors and elements is challenging and necessary at today's community college.

This book illustrates the many ways community colleges and their partners are working to support diverse groups of immigrants and refugees in their regions, representing various ethnicities, cultures, beliefs, as well as skill levels, ranging from those who have limited English proficiency and lack high school diplomas to those who arrive in the United States with college credentials and often years of professional experience. The promising practices in this volume come from Blue Ribbon Panel members of the Community College Consortium for Immigrant Education (CCCIE), a national network of leading community colleges and experts in the field committed to increasing educational and career opportunities for immigrant and refugee students and strengthening the capacity of the community colleges that serve them.

The American Association of Community Colleges (AACC) and the CCCIE have shared a mutually beneficial relationship since CCCIE's start in 2008, including the participation of AACC on CCCIE's Blue Ribbon Panel. Kevin Christian, director for diversity, inclusion, and equity, has represented AACC on the Consortium's panel and has contributed his expertise and knowledge to CCCIE's work over the years. CCCIE's collaboration with AACC has provided opportunities for the dissemination of CCCIE's initiatives among the nation's community colleges.

Diversity challenges are found at all organizations and sectors, not just higher education. But, knowing that community colleges serve the majority of minority college students in the United States, it is critical to develop a culture of inclusion in the community college environment. As community colleges continue to serve as open-access postsecondary institutions and the gateway to educational attainment, we must ensure that our institutions are fully versed in local, state, and national policies pertaining to access, completion, and student success issues.

This book provides practical models for change, illustrating how initiatives implemented to serve a growing, diverse immigrant student population not only reflect a college's commitment to diversity and inclusion, but also contribute toward—and, in fact, are critical to increasing—overall student retention, college completion, and employment outcomes.

It is vital that our colleges are vested in and committed to providing quality educational opportunities for all students. Community college administrators must be knowledgeable about and committed to institutions' and students' rights and responsibilities. In addition, cultural competence and sensitivity to the current landscape and changes that affect student populations are definitely skills that are required to be effective in this area. College administrators should be able to articulate the importance of equity and inclusion to the broader education mission not only of their institution but to higher education in general.

Diversity and inclusion officers cannot do it alone. The authors have provided a roadmap of promising practices and practical information for leveraging innovative immigrant and refugee education programs. These practices align with and strengthen the growing importance of student success initiatives, as well as the focus on diversity and inclusion on campus and beyond. Current and future leaders of community colleges will benefit from this work as they are called upon to lead critical conversations at their colleges and looked upon as role models in their community.

Walter Bumphus, president and CEO
American Association of Community Colleges

Preface

Teresita B. Wisell

In 1959, the Cuban Revolution unleashed the largest refugee flow in history to the United States, with more than half a million people fleeing the island over the fifteen years following the toppling of Fulgencio Batista by Fidel Castro's guerrilla fighters. Four years after the Revolution, in April 1963, my parents, my older sister, and I left our home in Camaguey, Cuba, with two suitcases. My sister was just shy of her fifth birthday. I was sixteen months old. Commercial flights between Cuba and the United States had been suspended after the Cuban Missile Crisis in October 1962, so we flew to Mexico City and lived there for several weeks, awaiting our visas to enter the United States.

We were blessed to have been one of a few Cuban families sponsored by an Episcopal church in Wilmington, Delaware. It was there that my parents started over—making a home for me, my sister, and the two younger brothers who would be born in the coming years. They, like thousands of Cuban refugees, expected to return to their native home. This was to be a temporary safe haven for their young family. But that was not to be. As we were growing up, my parents kept us connected as best they could with family and traditions—not easily accomplished without cell phones, the internet, or social media. Whereas most Cubans had immigrated to Miami, our family experienced its own diaspora—Chicago, Miami, Delaware, Puerto Rico, Spain, and, of course, those we left behind.

I did not grow up thinking I was an immigrant or a refugee, although I am both. As a child, I proudly stated I was a Cuban American, telling my friends and teachers that I was born in Cuba, spoke Spanish at home, and ate Cuban food. I was a novelty. I had no idea of the stress faced by my father as he searched for employment commensurate with his education or my mother as she supported my sister's entry to kindergarten at a time when English as a second language programs did not exist in the K–12 system, especially not in Delaware.

As we acclimated to our new surroundings, two principles became the pillars of our home. Nothing was more important than family and education. Our extended family was spread throughout the world; nonetheless, family would always come first. Moreover, while everything we owned had been taken from us, no individual or government had been able to take away my parents' education. It belonged to them. It would be what carried them forward in this new land that they would learn to call home. As a result, my parents were laser focused on supporting our educational success and taught us to take ownership of our academic journeys. The vibrancy of our own "American Dream" would depend on our persistence and dedication to learning. It's no surprise, then, that my mother finished her own education in the United States and became a teacher, and three of her children established our own careers in education.

For twenty-five years, I have had the privilege of being a community college administrator and educator—working in an academic sector that values access to education and training for all who are determined to work for it. Community colleges across the country are opening doors to individuals for whom education and training might not otherwise be available and giving them the tools they require to shape a successful future for themselves and their families. Nearly a third of the student population at community colleges nationwide come from immigrant backgrounds (Migration Policy Institute, October 2017, Current Population Survey, Education Supplement). Given our mission of access and our focus on creating pathways for educational and career advancement, community colleges are the most obvious sector of higher education to intentionally commit to immigrant student success.

Immigrants and children of immigrants are among those for whom community colleges can be transformative. It was with that understanding that Suzette Brooks Masters, then the program officer at the J. M. Kaplan Fund, joined with Westchester (New York) Community College to found the Community College Consortium for Immigrant Education (CCCIE). Since 2008, Westchester Community College has been committed to leading this national movement with a mission to expand the capacity of community colleges to accelerate immigrant and refugee success and raise awareness of the critical role that community colleges play in advancing immigrant integration. It is a recognition of the potential of immigrants to contribute to our communities, our economy, and our nation that has motivated the CCCIE network to advance this work and galvanize the community college sector in support of all members of our communities.

At the center of our work are five guiding principles. These five principles resonate throughout the chapters of this book and within the successful programs that we highlight here.

We believe in equity with excellence. We know that community colleges working together can do more to promote and advance immigrant education on a national scale than any one college can achieve on its own. As a network of leading colleges working to accelerate immigrant and refugee student success, CCCIE is committed to the open exchange of information and promising practices. Through shared learning and guidance, CCCIE works to achieve equal opportunity for New Americans to acquire the skills they need to thrive in a knowledge economy.

We recognize immigrants and refugees as assets to our communities and the nation. Immigrant and refugee students enhance the diversity of our campuses and contribute to our local and national economies. Providing access to higher education for immigrants is crucial not only for their personal success, but for the economic and cultural vibrancy of local communities and our country as well.

We are committed to partnerships. We also recognize that community colleges cannot advance the agenda for immigrant integration in their communities by working alone. As such, colleges thrive best when they operate as part of a broader ecosystem committed to building meaningful, multisector partnerships that encourage collaborators to leverage their resources in their respective areas of expertise. Openness in strategic conversations with all stakeholders is a critical building block for strong partnerships.

We support the successful completion of a student's intended goals. We recognize that immigrants may come to community colleges for a variety of reasons—to continue their education, get a job or advance their careers, improve their English, become stronger parent advocates, prepare for citizenship, or even to become entrepreneurs. Students are best served when colleges forge targeted, "intentionally focused" academic, career, and support plans around completion that allow individuals to fulfill their intended goals.

We believe in accountability. We believe colleges should articulate explicit, measurable goals to serve immigrant and refugee students and incorporate these as part of the college's overall strategic plan, backed up with resources and actions on the ground to make these strategies work. CCCIE is committed to building evidence-based cultures at our colleges; improving academic, workforce, and societal outcomes for our immigrant and refugee populations, and working across silos and sectors to create shared value.

It has been more than ten years since our founding and CCCIE remains firmly committed to our mission. It has been my privilege to lead the organization since its inception. This book captures the expertise and dedication of colleagues across the country in community colleges, community agencies, and nonprofit organizations who have joined us in our work. It is through our collective efforts that our immigrant and refugee students have found their success. My personal thanks to Jill Casner-Lotto, my colleague and friend. As director of CCCIE, Jill's talents and unwavering commitment have been instrumental in moving our agenda. She directed the writing of the case studies in this book and worked closely with the authors to help them shape the scope and content of their chapters. Together, we thank all the authors for sharing their work and making this book a reality.

I return to my beginning as we look to understand the future. I thank my parents for their courage and their vision for a better life through education. We each have an opportunity to pay it forward and this work has been mine.

Acknowledgments

The Community College Consortium for Immigrant Education (CCCIE) has advanced its agenda by building on the collective expertise and experiences of our member colleges as well as through strategic partnerships with several organizations, both within and outside the community college sector. First, we would like to thank the Blue Ribbon Panel (BRP) members who contributed chapters to this book. All of our BRP members represent CCCIE's "brain trust." They serve as CCCIE's ambassadors and advocates, helping us raise the visibility of immigrant education programs at national conferences, connecting with other community colleges to advance the field, and articulating the reasons these initiatives are essential to ensure that our communities thrive socially and economically. Their willingness to share their work and write candidly about the challenges and opportunities involved—on top of their busy "day jobs"—is commendable.

CCCIE came about in 2008 thanks to the vision and determination of several individuals. The late Joseph N. Hankin, former president of Westchester Community College, understood how CCCIE could project a national unified voice on the important role community colleges play in educational and career services for immigrants and gladly offered the college's generous support in leading a dynamic network to promote and exchange innovative models. Suzette Brooks Masters saw the potential for community colleges to be at the forefront of a national movement to strengthen immigrant education and successfully secured funding from the J. M. Kaplan Fund to provide major support for CCCIE over the following nine years. As president of Westchester Community College, Belinda S. Miles has continued the college's leadership role and helped launch CCCIE's College Presidents Campaign to engage additional community college presidents across the country in CCCIE's mission and sign onto our Presidents for New American Success Pledge.

CCCIE's collaboration with the American Association of Community Colleges (AACC) has provided a critical channel for disseminating our initiatives and elevating our work at the national level. We wish to thank AACC as the copublisher of this book, in recognizing the crucial role immigrants and refugees play in strengthening our country and the important work of community colleges to provide pathways to their educational and career success. We are especially grateful to Walter G. Bumphus, president and CEO of AACC, and Kevin Christian, AACC's director for diversity, inclusion, and equity, for their support.

Building and advancing the field of immigrant education and workforce development would be impossible without our multisector partnerships. We are grateful to the Kresge Foundation for its support to help CCCIE integrate its expertise on immigrant education issues into broader national college completion and workforce development initiatives. CCCIE's membership in the Immigrant Professional Integration (IMPRINT) coalition and our collaboration with World Education Services (WES) Global Talent Bridge have broadened our knowledge of immigrant professional integration and strengthened our work to help colleges and communities tap into the talents of foreign-educated immigrants and refugees. CCCIE participates in WES Global Talent Bridge's Skilled Immigrant Integration Program, which provides technical assistance to multisector teams across the country working together to help skilled immigrants better integrate into the economic and social fabric of their communities and the country.

CCCIE is also proud to be part of the Skills and Opportunity for the New American Workforce (SONAW) project, a multisector partnership led by the National Immigration Forum, with support from the Walmart Foundation's Opportunity Initiative. SONAW has opened new opportunities for immigrant retail workers and helped employers improve productivity through a scalable, worksite-based training model that integrates English-language learning with job-related skills, blending online and in-person instruction. Our collaborations with the National Council for Workforce Education and with the National Skills Coalition have enhanced CCCIE's crosscutting work at the intersection of immigrant education and workforce development. And, most recently, CCCIE's collaboration with the Presidents' Alliance on Higher Education and Immigration has strengthened our advocacy work in support of a bipartisan Development, Relief, and Education for Alien Minors (DREAM) Act and opposition to proposed "public charge" rule changes that would penalize low-income immigrant students and adult learners who access public benefits that are critical to ensuring they enroll and succeed in higher education and workforce training.

This book would not have come to fruition without the expert copyediting and organizational skills of Gail Robinson, a professional writer, editor, trainer, and program management consultant to nonprofit and higher education institutions. Additionally, as AACC's former director of service learning, she brought a keen appreciation for understanding the importance of civic engagement and the role it plays in immigrant education and integration. Her edits, attention to detail, and thoughtful observations about the book's overall content improved the manuscript significantly. Our sincere thanks also to Sarah Jubar, acquisitions editor for Rowman & Littlefield, for her patience, encouragement, and useful advice throughout this process.

Finally, we acknowledge the immigrant and refugee students themselves, for their persistence, agency, and determination to overcome obstacles and chart a path forward in contributing their talents and enriching our campuses, our communities, and our country. Thank you.

Introduction

Jill Casner-Lotto

A nurse from Ecuador, who left her professional career there more than a decade ago and faced significant language challenges in attempting to advance her career in the United States, enrolls in an innovative community college program providing English-language skills integrated with career training and test preparation. She is finally able to obtain her relicensure in the United States and practice as a full-time registered nurse in a healthcare facility.

Lower-skilled adult immigrant learners, who may lack high school diplomas, are able to enroll in affordable and accelerated education pathways that improve basic literacy and job skills, and also lead to employer-recognized certificates in high-demand fields. Immigrant students, working in teams alongside native-born students, engage in curriculum-based service-learning projects benefiting their communities. And refugees coming from Congo, Iran, Syria, and countries all over the world, who arrive with training and degrees from their home countries, learn how to navigate US job culture and transition to further education or professional jobs that align with their skills and experience.

Community colleges serve as a critical gateway to English-language instruction, higher education, workforce training, and civic engagement for many immigrants and refugees looking to gain an economic foothold in the labor market and integrate into the social fabric of their communities. At both ends of the educational and skills spectrum and coming from various walks of life with different goals and aspirations, immigrants and refugees have turned to community colleges to help them further their education, prepare for citizenship, or launch new careers. And although a growing number of community colleges have adopted a strategic approach that intentionally targets resources to support a highly diverse immigrant and refugee population, many colleges could strengthen their efforts to attract, enroll, and connect these students with the relevant resources and programs to plan a viable educational and career path in the United States. [1]

The Community College Consortium for Immigrant Education (CCCIE) was founded in 2008 on the belief that community colleges working together could do more to promote and advance immigrant education on a national scale than any one college could achieve on its own. CCCIE's commitment focuses on building community colleges' capacity to accelerate immigrant and refugee success and raising awareness of the essential role these colleges play in advancing immigrant integration in our communities. This book draws upon the knowledge and expertise of our national Blue Ribbon Panel (BRP) gained over the past decade to share the key lessons learned and personal perspectives of several BRP members representing colleges from various parts of the country; reflective narratives from partners who have collaborated with CCCIE are also included.

The purpose of our book is to bring leading-edge examples in immigrant/ refugee education, career development, and integration to public attention and to disseminate this knowledge to a wide audience of community college educators, workforce development decision-makers, policy experts, and other key stakeholders. At a time when our nation is facing bitter political divides over its immigration policies and gridlock at the federal level, this book tells a different story: it illustrates the exemplary initiatives of community colleges and their partners working together at local and state levels to integrate immigrants and refugees into the economic, social, and cultural fabric of our communities and country, and it illustrates the various ways immigrant and refugee students enrich campus life, strengthen communities, and benefit our economy and society.

As of this writing, Congress has failed to pass a bipartisan Development, Relief, and Education for Alien Minors (DREAM) Act that would provide permanent protections, federal financial aid eligibility, and a pathway to US citizenship for undocumented immigrant youth, known as Dreamers, who came to the United States as children, have built their lives here, and consider this country their home. However, the House of Representatives took a historic step forward in its passage of the Dream and Promise Act, H.R.6, in June 2019. This legislation is discussed later in this introduction. Community colleges have taken necessary steps to support educational and career opportunities for undocumented immigrant students, including those covered under the Deferred Action for Childhood Arrival (DACA) program, which, since 2012, has provided Dreamers with temporary protections and work authorization.

Despite the Trump administration's decision to end DACA in fall 2017, several federal court challenges have kept DACA in place temporarily.[2] However, without a permanent legislative solution providing an eventual path to citizenship, DACA recipients, as well as other undocumented immigrant youth and their families are currently living in limbo. Furthermore, as DACA recipients have become so well integrated into schools, colleges, communities, and workplaces throughout the country, the economic and social repercussions of ending DACA would be widespread and significant.[3]

IMMIGRANT AND REFUGEE EDUCATION: A CRITICAL NATIONAL IMPERATIVE

Our nation is now facing fundamental demographic shifts, with immigrants and their children expected to account for almost all workforce growth over the next two decades, as baby boomers retire and the population ages.[4] Yet about thirty million of these fifty-eight million immigrant-origin adults lack postsecondary credentials, which include education or training earned beyond high school, such as a college degree, apprenticeship certificate, professional certification, or occupational license, according to a 2019 Migration Policy Institute (MPI) report that provides the first-ever analysis of this population. These immigrant-origin adults (first- and second-generation immigrants) represent 30 percent of the one hundred million US adults ages sixteen to sixty-four who lack postsecondary credentials. Many first-generation immigrants face especially steep barriers to obtaining credentials: more than 60 percent without postsecondary credentials have limited English language proficiency, and almost one-third are unauthorized.[5]

At the same time, industry faces growing skills shortages, with an increased need for higher levels of training and education. Almost two in three jobs today require some form of postsecondary education or training.[6] Yet less than half of US adults ages twenty-five to sixty-four today actually meet those requirements. Immigrant-origin adults make up a large but often under-recognized population for focusing efforts to boost credential attainment, and those who have already obtained postsecondary credentials are making economic gains.[7]

The MPI report noted the significant labor-market value of nondegree credentials that had been earned by immigrant-origin adults regardless of their educational level: immigrant-origin adults holding certifications or licenses in occupations ranging from barbers to licensed practical nurses had higher levels of labor-force participation, higher incomes, and lower rates of unemployment than their counterparts who lack them. "Helping a significant share of these 30 million immigrant-origin adults obtain high-quality, marketable postsecondary credentials can become a critical tool in meeting national and state higher education attainment goals, addressing current and projected labor shortages, and raising labor productivity," the report coauthor and MPI senior fellow Michael Fix concluded.[8]

To meet the need for more skilled and educated workers, more than forty states have established ambitious goals for postsecondary credential attainment.[9] Demand for middle-skills jobs, requiring more than a high school diploma but less than a four-year degree, remains strong,[10] yet many states will find it difficult or impossible to reach their goals without including their immigrant residents, according to the National Skills Coalition.[11] Community colleges have increasingly aligned their own institutions' student completion goals with their state's higher education and workforce goals and realize the college and career success of their immigrant populations is critical to meeting those targets.

College-educated immigrants represent a major source of untapped talent that is especially critical given the labor and skills shortages cited in key fields such as healthcare, engineering, and technology. Almost half (48 percent) of immigrant adults who came to the United States between 2011 and 2015 were college graduates—a marked increase from the 33 percent among those who entered before the 2007–2009 recession and 27 percent who arrived before 1990, according to MPI. Yet, despite the sharply rising education level of recent US immigrants, many skilled immigrants remain unemployed or underemployed, working in low-wage, low-skill jobs. The collective "brain waste" experienced by both foreign- and US-educated immigrants is estimated to result in more than $39 billion in lost earnings and more than $10 billion in lost federal, state, and local taxes.[12]

PRACTICAL MODELS FOR CHANGE

Community colleges are well positioned to be critical change agents in improving educational and workforce access, increasing economic mobility, and ensuring a more equitable future for a diverse immigrant and refugee population, but they face significant challenges in adopting and sustaining programs that successfully align immigrant/refugee education initiatives into the college system as a whole. This book provides practical models for change, with an emphasis on what works, but also considers the critical challenges and lessons learned as college programs have evolved in response to student, employer, and community needs. It looks at how community colleges have overcome barriers and opened opportunities for significant change in the lives and economic prospects of immigrants and refugees.

CCCIE and its BRP members have made a commitment to the integration of immigrants and refugees in college life and in community and civic life in general. Successful linguistic, civic, and economic integration depends on visionary leadership at the top and participation of individuals from various levels and across divisions of the community college organization, as well as robust multisector partnerships with a diverse group of stakeholders, including community organizations, adult education systems, K–12 school districts, four-year institutions, employers, and workforce investment boards.

This book shares the perspectives of community college CEOs and the role of leadership in adopting institutional-wide strategies and allocating resources that have advanced immigrant and refugee integration on campus and in the community. We also learn how frontline practitioners make those strategies work through educational and career pathways that have enabled immigrants and refugees to pursue their academic and career goals and contribute to the economic prosperity and cultural vibrancy of their communities.

A companion volume, *Working Together: How Community Colleges and Their Partners Help Immigrants Succeed*, focuses on two additional key components of successful immigrant and refugee integration: multisector partnerships that have been essential for increasing students' college and career readiness and ensuring their transition to further education, training, or jobs; and strategies related to replicating and scaling best-practice models and the policy implications involved. We cite student voices and stories throughout both books.[13]

Collectively, the two texts provide a sampling of the innovative work in this constantly evolving field, and do not represent a comprehensive review of other successful community college initiatives making gains to promote the educational and workforce success of immigrants and refugees. The books feature initiatives of community colleges in both urban and suburban locations and include examples illustrating evidence-based approaches that support student retention, college and credential completion, employment, and economic mobility. Our hope is that other community colleges and their partners will use these experiences to generate dialogues on campus and in communities and take concrete actions to build and sustain this work over time.

BACKGROUND AND DEFINITION OF
KEY TERMS AND LEGISLATION

Immigrant Students versus International Students

The promising practices in this book focus primarily on "immigrant students" broadly defined as individuals who have left their home country and intend to settle permanently in the United States. First-generation immigrants are those with no US citizenship at birth, whereas second-generation immigrants include US-born citizens with at least one foreign-born parent. The immigrant population includes refugees and asylees, naturalized US citizens, lawful permanent residents (also known as *green-card holders*), and undocumented students. International students attend college with a temporary student visa, with the intent to return to their country of origin, although they may seek to adjust their status and continue to live, work, and study in the United States. Although both immigrant students and international students are nonnative English speakers with some common concerns, it's important for community college practitioners to understand the differences between these two groups of student populations to provide the advice and resources that meet their specific needs.

ESL Contextualized Career Pathways

Although there are many different types of career pathways, an *English as a second language (ESL)–contextualized career pathway* generally refers to a well-articulated sequence of education and training with multiple entry and exit points that allow individuals to advance over time to higher levels of education and employment in a given industry sector or occupation.[14] Community colleges have designed ESL-contextualized career pathway programs that integrate English-language instruction with job skills training to help ESL students simultaneously improve their English and obtain employer-recognized credentials in high-demand fields. Programs have been designed to serve immigrants coming from diverse educational backgrounds in their home countries, including those without high school diplomas and others with professional credentials and university degrees. ESL bridge programs or on-ramps have allowed beginning- or intermediate-level ESL learners to transition into ESL-contextualized career pathways, which may require more advanced English language skills.

Dream and Promise Act of 2019

First introduced as bipartisan legislation in 2001, the DREAM Act has since been introduced several times in Congress in various forms over the past two decades and most recently in March 2019. The Dream and Promise Act of 2019, passed by the House, represents a more expansive version of previous bills, including the bipartisan Dream Act of 2017, which has also been reintroduced in the Senate as the Dream Act of 2019.[15] The Dream and Promise Act would offer a path to legal status and citizenship, expand access to federal financial aid, and provide permanent protections for Dreamers (incluidng nearly 700,000 DACA recipients), as well as immigrants eligible for temporary protected status (TPS) and deferred enforced departure (DED), who have escaped difficult conditions, such as war or natural disasters, in their home countries.[16]

An estimated 2.7 million immigrants could receive permanent protections under the bill, including 2.3 million Dreamers, as well as nearly 430,000 TPS and DED recipients.[17] Dreamers would have to meet numerous requirements to be granted conditional permanent resident status and then be eligible for full lawful permanent resident status through either a higher education track or military service or employment. Educational requirements would include earning a degree from a US higher education institute or completing at least two years toward a bachelor's degree or earning a certificate from a postsecondary career and technical education (CTE) program. The legislation establishes a new grant program for noprofit organizations, including colleges, to help individuals gain protections and meet requirements of the bill. While the current Dream and Promise Act provides broader protections than previous versions of the Dream Act, unlike earlier versions it does not include repeal of a 1996 provision penalizing states that grant in-state tuition for undocumented students on the basis of residency.[18] Nonetheless, the legislation represents a major step forward in terms of its scope of coverage and its recognition of Dreamers and other undocumented immigrants as key contributors to communities and college campuses, as well as crucial participants in the US workforce and economy.[19]

Also critical are the two bipartisan Senate bills recently reintroduced: the Dream Act of 2019, which provides a path to citizenship for Dreamers and DACA recipients, and the SECURE Act, which would provide similar protections and a path to citizenship for TPS and DED recipients. Although prospects for passage of any of these bills remain unclear, their discussion and debate in Congress and increased advocacy could help build momentum for further bipartisan support.

Tuition-Equity Laws

Although many immigrant students face financial and other challenges in accessing higher education, undocumented students encounter especially steep obstacles when trying to access college, training, or jobs. They are ineligible for all federal financial aid—including grants, loans, and work study—and face a patchwork of in-state tuition and aid policies that vary state by state. Many live in fear of deportation and uncertainty about the future. As of this writing, twenty states have implemented tuition-equity laws allowing eligible undocumented youth to pay in-state tuition rates at public colleges, and twelve states offer state financial aid to undocumented students who meet certain criteria.[20] States that have passed tuition-equity laws have seen greater increases in postsecondary enrollment among DACA youth than states that have not implemented such laws, according to a National Bureau of Economic Research working paper.[21]

Deferred Action Childhood Arrival (DACA)

In the absence of a DREAM Act, the DACA program, implemented by the Obama administration in 2012, has provided about 700,000 eligible Dreamers temporary relief from deportation and work authorization for a period of two years, subject to renewal.[22] Several national surveys have shown that DACA recipients are making significant contributions to the economy and their communities, with the majority employed or enrolled in school.[23] A 2018 survey of more than 1,400 student scholars enrolled at community colleges and universities that partner with TheDream.US found that more than 70 percent of students were employed, and two-thirds (66 percent) were pursuing professional careers in medical, legal, and engineering fields. Yet in most states, DACA recipients or undocumented students are not eligible to apply for professional licenses.[24]

Pell Grants

The federal Pell Grant program targets financial aid to low-income students to promote access to postsecondary education. With the increased focus on reauthorization of the Higher Education Act (HEA) in 2019, workforce development and higher education advocates have recommended several measures that would expand Pell Grant support for nontraditional and underrepresented students, including immigrant students and adult ESL learners.

Students are only eligible for Pell Grants if they are enrolled in credit programs requiring six hundred hours over a minimum of fifteen weeks, which prevents many working nontraditional students from accessing noncredit shorter-term certificates. The bipartisan Jumpstarting Our Businesses by Supporting Students (JOBS) Act would modernize HEA by extending Pell Grants to students enrolled in quality short-term training programs that are part of a career pathway when applicable and lead to industry-recognized credentials, as well as meeting other qualifications.[25] Additionally, a recent report from the National Association of Student Financial Aid Administrators notes that expanding federal student aid to include support for eligible ESL instruction would greatly improve English language learners' access and success in higher education.[26]

Ability to Benefit

Another key provision of HEA is "Ability to Benefit" (ATB), which affects students who can benefit from a college education but who lack a high school diploma or general equivalency diploma (GED) equivalent. ATB can be used to allow students to qualify for federal Pell Grants for postsecondary education if they meet certain ATB requirements and are enrolled in an eligible career pathway program.[27] Yet there is a lack of awareness and clarity on how the ATB provision can be implemented on community college campuses and what constitutes an eligible career pathway program.[28]

Although ATB can be a powerful tool to increase accessibility and affordability of quality training and education for low-income adult students and youth, including ESL learners, it is currently underutilized and requires additional technical assistance for administrators, teachers, and students to understand how ATB can be used.[29] The Department of Education has convened educators, advocacy groups, and policy experts to hear recommendations of how ATB could be better leveraged to support GED-seeking adult students to obtain federal aid and enter career pathways.[30]

Workforce Innovation and Opportunity Act

The Workforce Innovation and Opportunity Act of 2014 (WIOA) is the federal law governing Title I employment and training programs and Title II adult education programs, which are implemented at the state level. The overall intent is to deliver a more job-driven approach to training and skills development by building stronger ties between employers, state and local workforce development boards, community colleges, labor unions, nonprofit organizations, youth-serving organizations, and state and local officials.[31] WIOA addresses the barriers to employment faced by low-income adults and youth, including those who have limited English proficiency; opens opportunities for states' greater use of sector partnerships and career pathway models; and places increased emphasis on accountability and performance outcomes.[32]

Both WIOA Titles I and II include opportunities for providing education, training, and career pathways for English-language learners and immigrants so that they can move into postsecondary education and jobs. However, the data indicate serious deficiencies in meeting the needs of individuals with limited English skills in both Title I and Title II systems. Whereas 10 percent of working-age US adults have limited English proficiency, less than 2 percent of individuals who receive Title I training services have limited English proficiency.[33] Similarly, the Title II system meets the needs of only 3.4 percent of the 43.7 million adults in the United States who lack a high school diploma or have limited English proficiency.[34]

Carl D. Perkins Career and Technical Education Act

Congress passed the latest version of the Carl D. Perkins Act in July 2018. The legislation, the Strengthening Career and Technical Education for the 21st Century Act, is the primary federal funding source for high schools, community colleges, and four-year institutions that prepare youth and adults, including immigrants, for jobs in local and regional economies. CTE funds can enable immigrant and other US workers to earn short-term and stackable credentials; gain experience through work-based learning, including internships and apprenticeships; and can also support ESL courses integrated into noncredit, job-specific CTE curricula.[35]

OVERVIEW OF CONTENTS

This book is divided into two parts. Part I, "Executive-Level Commitment: Developing an Immigrant Education Strategy and Making It Work," provides perspectives from top administrators at community colleges around the country. Part II, "Frontline Teams Dedicated to Success of New Americans: Designing Pathways to College and Careers," outlines innovative pathway strategies and choices to be made.

Part I examines how college leaders have demonstrated their commitment to supporting immigrant and refugee students through articulation of strategies and allocation of resources to implement those strategies. They illustrate how these strategies support student success and college completion initiatives, address local and statewide labor market needs, and strengthen the college's focus on diversity and inclusion.

Suzette Brooks Masters, a consultant on immigration and immigrant integration issues, begins with a reflective narrative based on her experience at the J. M. Kaplan Fund, which helped launch CCCIE. She discusses the founding and evolution of the CCCIE network to promote cutting-edge immigrant education programs, and suggests that its member colleges have often faced the same struggles as the immigrants they support. But she maintains the risks taken—by the colleges to model forward-looking practices and by immigrants to pursue their dreams against formidable odds—are changing America for the better.

In chapter 1, Westchester Community College president Belinda S. Miles discusses the importance of CCCIE's work at the national level. As president, she describes her multiple roles of promoting key partnerships and initiatives that address the needs and emphasize the strengths of English-language learners, fostering increased multicultural understanding on campus and in the community, and providing progressive and integrative leadership needed to navigate successfully in the dynamic environment of immigrant education.

In chapter 2, President Malou C. Harrison of Miami Dade College's Eduardo J. Padrón and North campuses, conveys highlights of the shared vision and action agenda that the college is forging to advance immigrant education in its community. The college is proactive, innovative, equity-minded, and purposeful in providing lifelong educational opportunities for its growing immigrant population while meeting the workforce needs of a dynamic local business sector.

A commitment to access and success of immigrant students is deeply embedded in LaGuardia Community College's history, mission, and operations; yet the campus has been hit particularly hard by actual or threatened changes in immigration law and policies and law enforcement practices. Chapter 3 describes how former president Gail O. Mellow and the college's senior leaders responded to these developments by strengthening and expanding the resources and support services available to advance the safety and well-being of students, their families, and the community.

In chapter 4, Chancellor Lee D. Lambert of Pima Community College (PCC) notes the profound language, literacy, and cultural challenges presented by meeting the education needs of immigrant and refugee populations. He emphasizes long-standing local support of immigrant and refugee communities, describes how PCC's adult education division and its refugee education program have helped these communities overcome hurdles, and posits the need to leverage existing community relationships creatively to support DACA students.

In telling the story of Highline College in chapter 5, former vice president Jeff Wagnitz and former Dean Rolita Flores Ezeonu examine how leadership commitment to immigrant education is supported through Highline's mission statement and core values, its mission fulfillment metrics, and its history of serving—and benefiting from the assets of—the college's newcomer communities. Their chapter includes a review of several initiatives that represent Highline's present-day response to the region's diverse immigrant and refugee population.

John Hunt opens part II, which focuses on career pathways, with a review in chapter 6 of LaGuardia Community College's Center for Immigrant Education and Training (CIET), which offers free, noncredit adult courses in English for speakers of other languages (ESOL) that are contextualized to meet the varied needs of a diverse immigrant community. CIET provides an Immigrant Family Literacy ESOL program to help parents navigate local school systems; assists immigrant healthcare professionals in recredentialing and relicensing processes through its New York City Welcome Back Center; and offers ESOL learners without high school diplomas a high school equivalency bridge to college and careers.

In chapter 7, Juan Carlos Aguirre and Matthew Hebbard provide insight into an accelerated Integrated Career Pathways program at South Texas College that boosts educational and employment opportunities for low-skilled adults and ESL learners, including an occupational skills award program. They also describe how a comprehensive dual-credit program has provided tuition-free college courses and accelerated degree completion for high-skilled undocumented students, including Dreamers and DACA recipients, by addressing financial barriers, providing academic counseling, and helping students deal with emotional stress.

PCC's Transition to US Workforce program offers a low-cost, replicable approach to provide support for foreign-educated immigrant and refugee residents who need assistance transitioning to college-level education and occupational training programs that lead to skilled jobs and a living wage. Chapter 8's authors, Adam Hostetter, Montserrat Caballero, Norma Sandoval, and Regina Suitt, illustrate how an immigrant college and career navigator works with retired volunteers to advise students on aspects of job readiness and college knowledge that apply specifically to immigrants.

In chapter 9, Donna Kinerney explores workforce readiness and career pathways in Montgomery College's workforce ESOL programs. Following the Maryland Integrated Basic Education and Skills Training model, non-credit instruction focuses on high-demand occupational areas; integrated curricula; employment, academic, and support services; meaningful partnerships; and labor market–recognized credentials to move people rapidly into entry-level employment. She reflects on lessons learned as the staff determines how to reenvision programs and courses to align with new regulations under the federal WIOA of 2014.

Chapter 10 features Northern Virginia Community College's American Culture and Language Institute and its part-time, workforce-contextualized ESL Career Readiness program. Cynthia Hatch makes the case for transitioning students to sector-specific content instruction via support-ESL classes, a learning lab, and tailored workplace training; as well as using data to evaluate, redesign, and tailor curriculum to improve training and target student and employer needs more effectively.

Heide Spruck Wrigley wraps up part II with a reflective narrative that presents characteristics of quality programs from the perspective of beginning nontraditional English-language learners who are participating or would like to participate in career pathway programs. She provides advice to career navigators and shares her thoughts on her work with foreign-born students; how they find their way with the help of family, employers, community organizations, and colleges; and the importance of honoring their stories.

The book concludes with recommendations for actions drawn directly from our authors' and member colleges' promising practices and lessons learned, and organized according to the principles of CCCIE's Presidents for New American Success Pledge.[36]

Collectively, these authors provide timely and relevant ideas, innovative models, and concrete steps for promoting opportunities for immigrants and refugees at community colleges and in the communities where they live, work, and thrive.

NOTES

1. "Expanding Educational and Career Opportunities for Immigrant Students at Community Colleges" (New York: Community College Consortium for Immigrant Education, 2015), https://www.cccie.org/wp-content/uploads/2010/09/cccie_%20survey%20summary_key%20 findings%202015.pdf and "National Survey on Increasing Opportunities for New Americans at Community Colleges," *CCCIE Survey Briefing*, Washington, DC, November 2015, https:// www.cccie.org/wp-content/uploads/2010/09/ cccie%20survey%20briefing%20presentation_2015.pdf.

2. Although the US Citizen and Immigration Services had stopped accepting first-time DACA applications as of fall 2017, several US district court orders have allowed existing DACA recipients to submit renewal applications. In late June 2019, the US Supreme Court announced it would review the federal court cases challenging the government's termination of DACA. For the latest updates on DACA, see https://www.nilc.org/issues/daca.

3. Nicole Prchal Svajlenka, Tom Jawetz, and Angie Bautisa-Chave, "A New Threat to DACA Could Cost States Billions of Dollars," Center for American Progress, July 21, 2017, https://www.americanprogress.org/issues/immigration/news/2017/07/21/436419/new-threat-daca-cost-states-billions-dollars.

4. Jeffrey S. Passel and D'Vera Cohn, "Immigration Projected to Drive Growth in U.S. Working-Age Population through at Least 2035," Pew Research Center, March 8, 2017, http:// www.pewresearch.org/fact-tank/2017/03/08/immigration-projected-to-drive-growth-in-u-s-working-age-population-through-at-least-2035.

5. Jeanne Batalova and Michael Fix, "Credentials for the Future: Mapping the Potential for Immigrant-Origin Adults in the United States," Migration Policy Institute (March 2019), https:/ /www.migrationpolicy.org/research/credentials-immigrant-origin-adults-united-states.

6. Anthony P. Carnevale, Tamara Jayasundera, and Artem Gulish, *America's Divided Recovery: College Haves and Have-Nots* (Washington, DC: Georgetown University Center on Education and the Workforce, 2016), https://cew.georgetown.edu/wp-content/uploads/Americas-Divided-Recovery-web.pdf.

7. Batalova and Fix, "Credentials for the Future."

8. "Amid U.S. Demand for Higher Skills and Education, Credentialing Immigrant-Origin Adult Workers Could Be Key," Press Release, Migration Policy Report, March 7, 2019, https:// www.migrationpolicy.org/news/credentials-immigrant-origin-adult-workers-US.

9. *Statewide Educational Attainment Goals: A Case Study* (Indianapolis: Lumina Foundation, 2018), https://www.luminafoundation.org/files/resources/01-statewide-attainment-goals.pdf. See also HCM Strategists, "States with Higher Education Attainment Goals," February 2019, http://strongernation.luminafoundation.org/report/2019/media/Attainment_Goal_state%20 rundown_021519.pdf.

10. "United States' Forgotten Middle," National Skills Coalition, accessed January 30, 2019, https://www.nationalskillscoalition.org/resources/publications/file/middle-skill-fact-sheets-2014/NSC-United-States-MiddleSkillFS-2014.pdf.

11. "Middle-Skills Credentials and Immigrant Workers: Texas' Untapped Assets," National Skills Coalition, https://www.nationalskillscoalition.org/resources/publications/file/Middle-Skill-Credentials-and-Immigrant-Workers-Texas-Untapped-Assets.pdf. See also Amanda Bergson-Shilcock, *At the Intersection of Immigration and Skills Policy: A Roadmap to Smart Policies for State and Local Leaders* (Washington, DC: National Skills Coalition, September 2018), https://www.nationalskillscoalition.org/resources/publications/file/At-the-intersection-of-immigration-and-skills-policy_web.pdf.

12. Jeanne Batalova, Michael Fix, and James D. Bachmeier, *Untapped Talent: The Costs of Brain Waste among Highly Skilled Immigrants in the United States* (Washington, DC: Migration Policy Institute, 2016), https://www.migrationpolicy.org/sites/default/files/publications/ BrainWaste-FULLREPORT-FINAL.pdf. The term "college-educated" immigrants in MPI's report refers to people who obtained a four-year college degree or higher.

13. We have used pseudonyms when sharing students' personal stories throughout the book.

14. "The Alliance for Quality Career Pathways Approach: Developing Criteria and Metrics for Quality Career Pathways—A Working Paper" (Washington, DC: Center for Law and Social

Policy, February 2013), https://www.clasp.org/sites/default/files/public/resources-and-publications/files/CLASP-The-AQCP-Approach-Feb-2013.pdf.

15. Christian Penichet-Paul, "Dream Act of 2019: Bill Summary," National Immigration Forum, March 28, 2019, https://immigrationforum.org/article/dream-act-of-2019-bill-summary.

16. "Summary of Dream and Promise Act of 2019 (H.R.6)," National Immigration Law Center, June 7, 2019, https://www.nilc.org/issues/immigration-reform-and-executive-actions-summary-of-dream-and-promise-act-of-2019.

17. Julia Gelatt, "More Than a Dream (Act), Less Than a Promise," Migration Policy Institute, March 2019, https://www.migrationpolicy.org/news/more-dream-act-less-promise.

18. Jailene Acevedo and Jose Magaña-Salgado, "The Dream and Promise Act and Implications for Higher Education," Presidents' Alliance on Higher Education and Immigration, June 17, 2019, https://www.presidentsimmigrationalliance.org/blog-post-hr6-higher-ed.

19. Amanda Bergson-Shilcock, "Dream and Promise Act Sends Clear Message: Middle Skills Are a Pathway to Citizenship," National Skills Coalition, March 26, 2019, https://www.nationalskillscoalition.org/news/blog/dream-and-promise-act-sends-clear-message-middle-skills-are-a-pathway-to-citizenship.

20. "Basic Facts about In-State Tuition for Undocumented Immigrant Students," National Immigration Law Center, last updated June 1, 2018, accessed March 26, 2018, https://www.nilc.org/issues/education/basic-facts-instate.

21. Elira Kuka, Na'ama Shenhav, and Kevin Shih, "Do Human Capital Decisions Respond to the Returns of Education? Evidence from DACA," National Bureau of Economic Research Working Paper No. 24315, February 5, 2018, http://elirakuka.weebly.com/uploads/1/0/0/6/10064254/kss_2018.2.5.pdf. See also Amanda Bergson-Shilcock, "New Data Shows Sizable Education, Workforce Payoff of Investing in Immigrant Dreamers," National Skills Coalition, March 5, 2018, https://www.nationalskillscoalition.org/news/blog/new-data-shows-sizeable-education-workforce-payoff-of-investing-in-immigrant-dreamers.

22. "Deferred Action for Childhood Arrivals (DACA) Data Tools," Migration Policy Institute, accessed March 14, 2019, https://www.migrationpolicy.org/programs/data-hub/deferred-action-childhood-arrivals-daca-profiles.

23. Tom K. Wong, Sanaa Abrar, Tom Jawetz, Ignacia Rodriguez Kmec, Patrick O'Shea, Greisa Martinez Rosas, and Philip E. Wolgin, "Amid Legal and Political Uncertainty, DACA Remains More Important Than Ever," Center for American Progress, August 15, 2018, https://www.americanprogress.org/issues/immigration/news/2018/08/15/454731/amid-legal-political-uncertainty-daca-remains-important-ever.

24. Jose Magana-Salgado, "In Their Own Words: Higher Education, DACA, and TPS," TheDream.US, October 2018, https://www.thedream.us/wp-content/uploads/2018/10/The-Dream.US-In-Their-Own-Words-Report-Oct-2018-1-2.pdf.

25. "Make Pell Work: Pass the JOBS Act," National Skills Coalition, March 2019, https://www.nationalskillscoalition.org/action/take-action/body/Make-Pell-Work_Pass-the-JOBS-Act.pdf. See also Katie Brown, "Putting Pell Grants to Work for Working Students: How Modernizing Our Federal Higher Education Policy Can Improve Outcomes for Students and Employers in Today's Economy," National Skills Coalition, March 2018, https://www.nationalskillscoalition.org/resources/publications/file/Putting-Pell-Grants-to-work-for-working-students-1.pdf.

26. The Higher Education Committee of 50, "Innovative, Forward Thinking Recommendations to Congress on Higher Education Policy," National Association of Student Financial Aid Administrators, 2019, http://www.highereducationcommitteeof50.org/uploads/HEC50_Final_Report.pdf.

27. Lauren Walizer and Judy Mortrude, "Federal Guidance Explains How the Ability to Benefit Provision Aligns with a Career Pathway," Center for Law and Social Policy, May 19, 2016, https://www.clasp.org/blog/federal-guidance-explains-how-ability-benefit-provision-aligns-career-pathway.

28. David Baime, "Washington Watch: Seeking Guidance on 'Ability-to-Benefit' Rules," *Community College Daily*, American Association of Community Colleges, September 25,

2018, http://www.ccdaily.com/2018/09/washington-watch-seeking-guidance-ability-benefit-rules.

29. Lauren Walizer and Judy Mortrude, "Could 2019 Be the Year of ATB?" Center for Law and Social Policy," February 5, 2019, https://www.clasp.org/blog/could-2019-be-year-atb.

30. "Pima Leads the Way in Arizona," Pima Community College, Adult Basic Education for College and Career," March 15, 2019, https://pccadulted.wordpress.com/2019/03/15/pima-leads-the-way-in-arizona.

31. "The Workforce Innovation and Opportunity Act—Final Rules: A Detailed Look," US Department of Labor, accessed February 11, 2019, https://www.doleta.gov/WIOA/Docs/Final-Rules-A-Detailed-Look-Fact-Sheet.pdf.

32. "Workforce Innovation and Opportunity Act," National Skills Coalition, accessed February 11, 2019, https://www.nationalskillscoalition.org/federal-policy/workforce-investment-act.

33. Amanda Bergson-Shilcock, *Upskilling the New American Workforce: Demand-Driven Programs That Foster Immigrant Worker Success and Policies That Can Take Them to Scale*, (Washington, DC: National Skills Coalition, June 2016), https://www.nationalskillscoalition.org/resources/publications/file/Upskilling-the-New-American-Workforce-1.pdf.

34. Margie McHugh and Catrina Doxsee, *English Plus Integration: Shifting the Instructional Paradigm for Immigrant Adult Learners to Support Integration Success*, Migration Policy Institute, October 2018, https://www.migrationpolicy.org/research/english-plus-integration-instructional-paradigm-immigrant-adult-learners.

35. Zuzana Cepla, "Fact Sheet: What Is the Perkins CTE, and How Does It Serve Immigrants?" National Immigration Forum, July 25, 2018, https://immigrationforum.org/article/fact-sheet-perkins-cte-serve-immigrants.

36. "Presidents for New American Success Pledge," Community College Consortium for Immigrant Education, accessed March 20, 2019, https://www.cccie.org/wp-content/uploads/2016/07/CCCIE-Presidents-for-New-American-Success_Pledge_2016.pdf.

Part One

Executive-Level Commitment: Developing an Immigrant Education Strategy and Making It Work

Chapter One

Managing the New Normal

Presidential Leadership for Effective Community College Immigrant Education Programs

Belinda S. Miles

For generations, community colleges in large cities across the United States have enjoyed an influx of immigrants into their communities, with evidence suggesting an expansion of this trend. In the last fifty years, fifty-nine million people have immigrated to the United States, which holds one-fifth of the world's immigrants—exceeding by far any other country.[1] Emerging destinations tend to be metropolitan areas with more recent development histories, which are largely suburban in form.[2] Immigrants are moving beyond traditional gateway cities like New York, Los Angeles, Miami, Chicago, and San Francisco toward suburbs of large metropolitan areas like these and other new destinations in the southeast.[3]

Westchester County in New York is one such place. Just north of New York City, the county of nearly one million[4] is situated within a vibrant tristate metropolitan area of nineteen million residents[5] with substantial industry presence. The region boasts some factors cited in a study supported by the New York Immigration Coalition that determine how welcoming a city is to immigrants: access to an office of immigrant and new American affairs, access to a municipal identification program, affordable public transit, average cost of living, higher than average minimum wage, universal preschool, and good high school graduation rates.[6] In 2018, Westchester County government enacted the Immigrant Protection Act, extending the county's status as a place for "healthy integration of immigrants into local communities."[7]

The county's immigrant population is diverse. They are primarily from Spanish-speaking countries with 56 percent from Latin America and the rest from a variety of nations.[8] The most represented countries include Mexico (10 percent), Jamaica (7 percent), Dominican Republic (7 percent), and Ecuador (7 percent).[9] Westchester Community College (WCC) serves many individuals with high levels of education and skills but whose needs focus more on language acquisition and cultural immersion, as well as many who need intensive English-language skill development and workforce training.

For immigrants to engage fully in US civic life, education is a key factor.[10] Throughout generations, churches, settlement houses, community-based organizations, and similar establishments have served to welcome and acclimate immigrants to US communities and prepare them for workforce and civic engagement.[11]

A large part of my leadership commitment is to ensure that community colleges serve as a venue for helping individuals desiring to prepare for skilled and professional workforce participation and meaningful civic engagement. My personal lineage includes both Native Americans and nonimmigrant newcomers to America who experienced uneven access to education and its benefits. Experiences that support productive acclimation were limited.

As a first-generation African American college student, my work-study assisting students through tutoring at an open-access university reinforced in me the worth of programs and services that educate and uplift. Now in my second community college presidential role, I find that our work in immigrant education at WCC extends this legacy of service and commitment to talent development. I invite presidents similarly committed to join me and other colleagues in pledging support for our institutions' engagement in quality immigrant education programs.[12]

WCC's story began in 1946, just one year before the release of the landmark report of the President's Commission on Higher Education. That report marked a turning point in the history of community colleges, and it reminds us that community colleges have always adapted to changes around them to remain relevant. Among the commission's legacy is the characterization of the nation's community colleges as gateways to opportunity serving diverse communities with a primary mission of educational access.[13] We honor the "open door" access mission and respond to real issues occurring around us in real time.

At WCC, we have held a long-standing commitment to immigrant education to continuously meet the needs of the changing demographics of our county. In 2010, WCC opened the Gateway Center to serve as a central starting point for new Americans. Providing intentional support to this population transitioned the college from being a gatekeeper of educational and workforce opportunities to becoming a bridge builder. Despite competing priorities and the importance of meeting the needs of all community college students, we saw support for immigrant students as an urgent matter, in part, because of the opportunity to address anticipated labor force vacancies.

Community colleges with effective immigrant education programs often enjoy strong presidential leadership, with individuals at the helm capable of integrating various community resources with college needs and services. Founding Community College Consortium for Immigrant Education (CCCIE) presidents and chancellors such as Eduardo Padrón, Gail Mellow, and Lee Lambert are among those who often go beyond the pragmatism of the day-to-day management of running their colleges in a "business as usual" manner. Rather, they are expert synthesizers who regularly exhibit a distinct set of qualities on behalf of organizations where the constant evolution of myriad kinetic factors is the new normal.

Rapidly changing student demographics, emergent and unknown industries with novel job functions and work patterns, unexpected community partners, and unpredictable regulatory policies challenge today's community colleges to restructure many core services and work differently to serve the students we are receiving. Progressive and integrative leadership from community college presidents is needed to navigate successfully in the dynamic environment of continually expanding demand and need for immigrant education. This chapter describes five such abilities important for these leaders:

1. Connecting the dots: Gathering and synthesizing varied and disparate data points and trends to understand community needs

2. Vision: Making predictions about and building appropriate service models to meet identified needs

3. Collaboration: Bringing different community entities into effective partnerships on behalf of goals they have in common

4. Capacity building: Identifying, directing, and supporting innovative programming and the "frontline" individuals responsible for designing and executing effective programs

5. Advocacy: Courage to speak truth to power in shaping and responding to policies

CONNECTING THE DOTS

Many would agree that the twenty-first century is characterized by an ever-increasing atmosphere of scrutiny and accountability buttressed by seemingly infinite sources of data. Smartphones and other computing devices span all nations, generations, and multiple learning levels, making data availability ubiquitous and impossible to ignore. Analyzing, integrating, and prioritizing varied sources of information and "connecting the dots" to make such input meaningful and actionable is a cornerstone of the work we do at WCC and has been a vital part of our immigrant education programming. As the American College President 2017 Survey indicates, "Presidents must artfully combine their wisdom with data and analytics to make better decisions that improve the institution and boost student outcomes."[14]

Approaching its seventy-fifth anniversary in 2021, WCC has a long-standing history of meeting community needs through relevant college services. WCC was established to serve residents of diverse backgrounds. Among early enrollees at the college were returning World War II vets; women who delayed entry to higher education; low-income, first-generation college students; and many others. The college provided further access beginning in 1994 through local extension centers serving residents in five of the county's largest cities: Yonkers, White Plains, Mount Vernon, Peekskill, and Ossining.

In 1999, the Hitachi Foundation issued a "Corporate Citizenship Initiative" request for proposals, seeking projects that would produce partnerships with corporations designed to alleviate a particular societal problem. In response, cognizant of the rapidly rising numbers of new immigrants in Westchester County and in the student body, the WCC Foundation proposed a study to address how to better integrate new immigrants into the workplace. The proposal also suggested partnering with local businesses and community organizations to implement program goals. The grant initiative, known as the *New Immigrant Worker Project*, successfully:

- Moved the subject of educating immigrant workers high on the agendas of employers, educators, and government officials.
- Singled out workplace training as critical for immigrant workers' advancement.
- Identified proficiency in English, cross-cultural competency, adaptation to American workplace expectations, and basic computer and math skills as essential elements in workplace training.
- Identified small- to midsize businesses as the primary sector to target for workplace training because that sector employs such a large percentage of immigrant workers.

The project culminated with a regional leaders' conference, Preparing Tomorrow's Workforce 2007, where former deputy director of the Center for an Urban Future, Tara Colton, stated:

> Immigrants still come to New York with their hopes, their dreams, and their willingness to work hard to make them come true. But in the knowledge economy of the [twenty-first] century, that's not enough. English-language skills are much more important for this generation of immigrants than was the case for their predecessors. Without the ability to communicate with employers, co-workers, and customers, newcomers "hit the wall" of upward advance-

ment far more often and much more quickly than was true 100 or even 50 years ago. [15]

Today, we speak of "two Westchesters." Westchester County readily invokes images of wealth. According to the US Census Bureau, Westchester's average family income is $137,881 [16] and the median home value is $507,300. [17] Crain's New York [18] and the Tax Foundation [19] list the county among the highest taxed counties in the United States. A lesser-known but growing dynamic is the juxtaposition of poverty accounting for 9.8% of the population, [20] which characterizes the "other Westchester." [21]

In addition to financial challenges, many Westchester County immigrants who are part of this "other Westchester" also face language and education limitations. Our county's rich diversity includes immigrants and English-language learners, with one-quarter being foreign-born and one-third speaking a language other than English at home. [22] Among immigrants twenty-five years and older in Westchester County, nearly 24% have not graduated from high school. [23]

These local demographics are related to changes at the national level. In 2016, the Hispanic or Latino labor force reached 26.8 million nationwide. [24] In 2015, the Pew Charitable Trusts reported that "nationally, immigrants are more likely than the native-born population to be employed in industries that account for 29% of our nation's gross domestic product and employ 37% of our workers." [25] The American Action Forum projects that by 2020, the United States will be short an estimated 7.5 million private sector workers across all skill levels. [26]

The American Immigration Council states that "baby boomer retirements will create a need for almost fifty-seven million workforce replacements from 2010 to 2030 in all occupations and industries across the skills spectrum" and that "immigrants and their children are vital to replenishing the workforce as there would otherwise be a labor force deficit of millions of workers if only native-born (and not of immigrant parents) enter the workforce from 2010 to 2030." [27] Additionally, it is estimated that by 2030 the primary labor force population will experience a net loss of fifteen million whites while gaining twenty-six million racial minorities at the same time. [28]

Further, educational attainment plays a critical role in virtually every labor market, with a college degree being the most significant source of education or training for six of the ten fastest-growing occupations. [29] According to a Georgetown University study, "in recent years, the economy has shifted from one driven by high school–educated labor to one in which almost two in three jobs require some form of postsecondary education or training." [30] Relatedly, WCC collaborated with J. P. Morgan Chase Foundation and the New York City Labor Market Information Service to produce a report on the "middle skills" marketplace in the Lower Hudson Valley, highlighting promising career paths that require more than a high school diploma but less than a baccalaureate for entry.[31]

In 2011, WCC met Hispanic-serving institution (HSI) eligibility requirements, which require that an institution of higher learning enrolls Hispanic students at rates of 25 percent or higher.[32] The college became the State University of New York (SUNY) system's first to receive the US Department of Education's HSI designation. Colleges with this designation are eligible to participate in a competitive grant process providing funds to expand capacity to serve Hispanic and other low-income students. Current enrollment data at WCC indicate more than one-third of our enrollment population as of Hispanic origin.

In aggregate, these data points demand attention and indicate tremendous opportunity for targeted programs to meet these changing local needs. This is work for community colleges.

VISION

Although data is sometimes associated with lulling reviewers into a state of "analysis paralysis"—the experience of overanalyzing and interpreting without activity—it also has the power to stir within readers a call to action to bring about necessary change. Community college presidents must have the ability to lead teams that can make data actionable on behalf of institutional mission and on behalf of those whom the organization serves.

In some instances, simply looking at models developed by others is helpful. Best practices by the same or similar organizations are a great starting point for designing services to improve outcomes for targeted groups. It is important to recognize, however, that one size does not always fit all. Successful programs in large urban settings may be difficult to replicate in suburban or rural environments. Different funding mechanisms for immigrant education programming or differential access to community partners can also be inhibiting factors.

Where no models exist, new ones must be developed. This requires the ability to engage in a measured gap analysis between current and desired states and put together interventions designed to achieve the targeted outcome or status. Formative evaluation to assess progress toward goals enables retooling of programming, if needed. It also contributes to continuous improvement for maximum effectiveness.

In 2000, the WCC board of trustees and foundation began a more intentional focus on service to the new influx of immigrants into the county. At that time, demand for quality English as a second language (ESL) instruction far outpaced the supply, with the college's English Language Institute experiencing waiting lists. The previously mentioned Hitachi study and its culminating "Preparing Tomorrow's Workforce" conference heralded the advent of a new and expanded way to provide immigrant education.

The Gateway Center was the result of that focus. Inspired by the college's commitment to a more accessible education for recent immigrants to Westchester County and by the commitment of our county to serve all its residents, it is the largest partnership of public and private funding ever undertaken by the college and evidence of the critical role that philanthropy plays in access and equity initiatives. The Gateway Center was a newly constructed and iconic building that serves as a physical embodiment of the word "gateway"—an entrance or means of access. The center intentionally includes programs and services for both longtime residents and new Americans, bringing together all students and the community at large. Programming within the center includes the following:

- Modern language and ESL instruction
- International student services and an Immigrant Student Access Center
- Business programs and employer customized training
- A volunteer center featuring an extensive program of conversation partners

Other Gateway-based programs such as a Welcome Center, financial literacy, and entrepreneurship education also offer unique services to the immigrant community. Additional programming includes workshops providing legal and policy information to undocumented and Deferred Action for Childhood Arrivals (DACA) students and information sessions to support foreign-educated and skilled immigrants into career reentry. Another initiative connected to the center is the Kathryn W. Davis Global Community Scholars program, which engages many immigrant students by linking ten foreign-born and ten domestic students in curriculum-based service learning projects.

COLLABORATIVE PARTNERSHIPS

Community colleges are no strangers to connecting with neighboring institutions. Partnerships with local organizations to support immigrant education are a natural extension of what community colleges do well. The experience of connecting effectively with feeder high schools through targeted pipeline programs, as well as the hand-off of graduates to receiving institutions via carefully designed articulation agreements, develop within community colleges the skills needed to craft memoranda of understanding (MOU) with neighborhood organizations that support immigrant education programs.

One example is WCC's partnership with a local immigrant-serving organization, Neighbors Link. Through extensive collaboration, the college provides ESL classes, workforce training, and a pathway to postsecondary education to thousands of county residents. Similarly, the Neighbors Link Law Practice provides legal services to our immigrant students and their families. Montes and Choitz credit immigrant-serving organizations as places that "know, understand, and are trusted by immigrants and have long-standing expertise in providing appropriate and necessary supports."[33] These relationships just make good sense.

Beyond simply fashioning the MOU, other skills and behaviors contribute to successful partnerships. Being open to learning about each other, establishing clear contacts, and encouraging face-to-face meetings for better relationship building are a few recommended practices to strengthen partnerships among community colleges and immigrant-serving organizations.[34] Where such skills are lacking, professional development should be provided.

CAPACITY BUILDING

Assembling the right teams and determining the most effective operations to achieve a stated goal or set of tasks is an ongoing presidential task. The complexity of assignments involved in immigrant education programs is no exception. Individuals with a wide range of knowledge and the ability to span boundaries are needed to develop structures, content, and operations to support academic programming that achieves the desired teaching and learning objectives for effective immigrant education programs.

Instructional team members must have expertise in content development based on proven research and results. Many immigrant education programs focus on improving English-language acquisition as well as cultural acclimation and workforce preparation. WCC offers a robust English Language Institute with six levels of study, as well as specialized courses. The curriculum was designed and is updated based on comprehensive reviews of programming offered at various institutions across the nation as well as recommendations from the most current Teaching English as a Second Language (TESOL) literature and associations. Faculty have earned master's degrees or specialized certificates in TESOL and are trained in teaching methodologies that transcend a range of cultural differences and learning styles.

The ability to establish or reach appropriate key performance targets ensures that desired outcomes can be measured. Each year WCC serves about five thousand students in its English Language Institute who hail from more than one hundred countries speaking fifty languages. Our team of administrators and more than one hundred faculty work to help students progress through the curriculum with an eye toward entry to employment, advanced job opportunities, or college study. Noncredit-to-credit articulation is an important performance indicator, and we continuously retool programming to enhance the pipeline to higher learning and employment.

SPEAKING TRUTH TO POWER

Both standard and significant for community college presidents is the role of institutional advocacy. Whether through annual budget processes, capital campaigns, fund-raising, or policy input and response, this is an area of engagement requiring considerable strategy and effort. Support for immigrant education programs commands a place on this priority list.

Federal immigration policies can have an effect on community college immigrant education policies either positively or negatively. The Illegal Immigration Reform and Immigrant Responsibility Act (IIRIRA), enacted in 1996, instituted certain restrictions on states' residency requirements and in-state tuition benefits for postsecondary education, with negative repercussions for unauthorized immigrant students.[35]

As of this writing, Congress has yet to enact a bipartisan Development, Relief, and Education for Alien Minors Act that would repeal those restrictive provisions and also offer eventual lawful permanent residence and American citizenship that would benefit DACA students and other immigrant youth enrolled in postsecondary education.[36] Since it was first announced in June 2012, the DACA program has provided more than 800,000 undocumented youth temporary relief from deportation and the ability to study and work legally in the United States.

A 2018 national survey that analyzed the experiences of more than one thousand DACA recipients showed that nearly all were currently employed or enrolled in school, and were making significant contributions to the economy and their communities.[37] Yet it's been estimated that hundreds of thousands of individuals of the 1.8 million who would be potentially eligible for DACA continue to lose that opportunity as a result of the termination of the DACA program in September 2017.[38]

WCC was among those colleges and universities that offered professional development to faculty and staff about the status of the termination of the DACA program, and provided students with social and psychological support.[39] Several federal court challenges have kept DACA in place temporarily.[40] But in the absence of a permanent legislative solution and in the face of ongoing uncertainty of the DACA program, continuing professional development activities and information sessions will be necessary to keep faculty, staff, and counselors up to date on the changing legal landscape and help students deal with these persistent challenges.

Different states in the nation implemented their own actions in order to correct the absence of guidance to implement the IIRIRA. As of June 2018, twenty states offered in-state tuition to undocumented students: California, Colorado, Connecticut, Florida, Hawaii, Illinois, Kansas, Kentucky, Maryland, Minnesota, Nebraska, New Jersey, New Mexico, New York, Oklahoma, Oregon, Rhode Island, Texas, Utah, and Washington. Additionally, as of this writing, twelve states offered state financial aid to undocumented students: California, Colorado, Illinois, Maryland, Minnesota, New Jersey, New Mexico, New York Oklahoma, Oregon, Texas, and Washington.[41]

At the state level, presidents should monitor funding sources and speak out when changes affect local programs. Immediately upon my arrival at WCC in January 2015, revised state guidelines were being implemented that would eliminate funding for the lowest levels of ESL programs across the SUNY system. This funding policy change would negatively affect thousands of adults in our service area who required English instruction before charting a path to other opportunities for postsecondary education and workforce training. I felt that the new policy was akin to building half a bridge to which some of our neediest community members were expected to swim.

As the president of the SUNY system's first and only HSI at the time, I had to respond. I did so while simultaneously navigating my entry into a political landscape where our students, local community groups, state higher education system, and state and county legislators all had a significant stake.

Three years later, the story continues to evolve. We were able to mitigate some of the reduction in state aid for the lowest levels of ESL, while also using the opportunity to refine our curriculum and improve our metrics toward college readiness and entrance. Additionally, this occasion of speaking truth to power provided an opportunity to enlighten our system about changing demographics in our community likely to affect other regions of the state. Indeed, since that time, other SUNY institutions have reached or are rapidly approaching HSI status as they serve the broad range of English language learners in their communities.

Our commitment to the local immigrant community is reflected nationally through our college's role as the host institution for the CCCIE. The CCCIE is an important vehicle through which our sector has stepped out as a leader in the national arena on the topic of immigrant education. The Consortium's mission is to raise awareness of community colleges' role in immigrant and refugee integration through education and training, sharing best practices, and providing technical assistance to increase community colleges' capacity to deliver effective immigrant education programming.

Among CCCIE's successful efforts to date is the establishment of its Blue Ribbon Panel comprising senior community college leaders and experts in the field of immigrant education.[42] The panel has been effective at promoting partnership development and advocacy to advance immigrant education programs and policies.[43]

At WCC, CCCIE has provided opportunities to collaborate with national entities such as the National Immigration Forum, resulting in the delivery of ESL instruction and citizenship education into businesses throughout the county—meaningful work that was recognized by the White House in 2014 as the college received a "Champion of Change" award. In another initiative, CCCIE has partnered with the Forum, Miami Dade College, and the Walmart Foundation's Opportunity Initiative in the design and implementation of an innovative project to increase language and job-related skills among retail workers for whom English is a second language. The project has delivered contextualized ESL training at several community college sites, including WCC. The CCCIE's leadership extends into teaching and learning as evidenced by the award of a National Endowment for the Humanities grant to WCC for the creation of a Humanities Institute that embeds the immigrant experience into its curriculum.

Community college presidents can play a critical role in speaking truth to power in an effort to maximize benefits for students and their institutions by reviewing policies under consideration (preferably while being developed) and providing input, corresponding with public officials to make position statements regarding effects of potential regulations, sharing student profiles and individual testimonies to bring students' stories to life for those making determinations about their educational experiences, and providing relevant data regarding student experiences.

One president, albeit from a liberal arts college not funded by public resources, discussed college presidents breaking the "code of silence" and speaking out on politics in times when "statements or proposals in the political realm come into direct conflict with or openly threaten the educational missions of our institutions" indicating that "in such cases, silence is not prudence but an avoidance of the risk and responsibility that accompany the acceptance of a college presidency."[44] Still, prudence and emotional intelligence should be used as barometers for presidents to self-regulate, to know just how much to push or pull in order to "live to fight another day" versus digging in too deep and fighting the kind of battle that can leave you or your institution severely damaged.[45]

LESSONS LEARNED

Looking ahead, the need for continued presidential engagement and leadership for strong immigrant education programs seems ongoing. Like WCC, many of our peer institutions are committed to broad-based diversity, equity, and inclusion plans. Ours includes specific steps to enhance faculty, staff, and student experiences through the lens of diversity, equity, and inclusion.[46]

WCC's plan outlines roles for stakeholders and partners to collaboratively work to increase and sustain diverse faculty, staff, and administrators and to establish a climate of cultural consciousness and competence. We also take a critical look at the student experience and commit to addressing achievement gaps and inclusive support services. My 2018 appointment to a newly established county Minority and Women Business Enterprise Task Force[47] provides an additional area of focus for this work.

We recognize our immigrant education efforts as both an investment in people and an economic imperative. We have studied in-depth the demand for employees educated for the growing number of middle-skill jobs in our region. We remain vigilant in our efforts to provide access to opportunity as we work to close the gap between our available graduates and these workforce opportunities. That workforce is increasingly multicultural and multilingual. Our immigrant education programs must be multifaceted and effective for us to achieve this end. Community college presidential leadership can help ensure viable programming in this area to meet this ongoing need and effectively manage this new normal.

NOTES

With gratitude, I acknowledge the contributions of Dr. Shawn Brown, Dr. Carmen Martínez-López, Ms. Tiffany Hamilton, and Ms. Jessica Tagliaferro to this chapter.

1. "Modern Immigration Wave Brings 59 Million to US Driving Population Growth and Change through 2065: Views of Immigration's Impact on US Society Mixed," *Pew Research Center Hispanic Trends* (Washington, DC: Pew Research Center, September 2015), http://www.pewhispanic.org/2015/09/28/modern-immigration-wave-brings-59-million-to-u-s-driving-population-growth-and-change-through-2065/.

2. Audrey Singer, "The New Geography of United States Immigration," *Brookings Immigration Series*, no. 3 (Washington, DC: Brookings Institution, July 2009), https://www.brookings.edu/wp-content/uploads/2016/06/07_immigration_geography_singer.pdf.

3. Singer, "The New Geography."

4. US Census, American Community Survey 5-Year Estimates, Table DP05, 2016, http://factfinder.census.gov.

5. US Census, *American Community Survey, Table DP05*, 2016, http://factfinder.census.gov.

6. "The Ten Best Cities for Immigrants in the US," *TransferWise*, November 27, 2017, accessed on August 27, 2018, https://transferwise.com/us/blog/10-best-cities-us-immigrants.

7. "Immigration Protection Act," Neighbors Link, accessed July 21, 2019, https://www.neighborslink.org/issues/immigrant-protection-act.

8. "FAQs about the Immigrant Community in Westchester County," *Neighbor's Link*, accessed August 27, 2018, https://www.neighborslink.org/issues/immigration-northern-westchester.

9. "FAQs about the Immigrant Community in Westchester County." *Neighbor's Link*, accessed August 27, 2018, https://www.neighborslink.org/issues/immigration-northern-westchester.

10. "Immigrants and Higher Education," *AAC&U News*, October 2015, accessed August 23, 2018, https://www.aacu.org/aacu-news/newsletter/immigrants-and-higher-education.

11. "Aspiration, Acculturation, and Impact: Immigration to the United States, 1789–1930," *Harvard University Library Open Collections Program*, accessed August 24, 2018, http://ocp.hul.harvard.edu/immigration/settlement.html.

12. "Join the Pledge," *Community College Consortium for Immigrant Education*, accessed August 26, 2018, https://www.cccie.org/presidents-pledge/join-the-pledge.

13. Philo A. Hutchesen, "The Truman Commission's Vision of the Future," *Thought & Action: The NEA Higher Education Journal* 4 (2007), https://www.nea.org/assets/img/Pub-ThoughtAndAction/TAA_07_11.pdf; Claire Gilbert and Donald Heller, "The Truman Commission and Its Impact on Federal Higher Education Policy," (Working Paper No. 9, University of Pennsylvania Center for the Study of Higher Education, 2010), https://ed.psu.edu/cshe/working-papers/wp-9.

14. *American College President Survey 2017*, American Council of Education and TIAA Institute (New York: TIAA Institute, June 2017).

15. Tara Colton, Jason Fischer, and Jonathan Bowles, eds., *Policy Brief* (New York: Center for an Urban Future and the Schuyler Center for Analysis and Advocacy, November 2006).

16. US Census, *American Community Survey 5-Year Estimates, Table DP03*, 2016, http://factfinder.census.gov.

17. US Census, *American Community Survey 5-Year Estimates, Table DP04*, 2016, http://factfinder.census.gov.

18. "New York Commuter Counties Top List for Highest Property Taxes," *Crain's New York Business*, April 5, 2018, http://www.crainsnewyork.com/article/20180405/REAL_ESTATE/180409947/new-york-commuter-counties-top-list-for-highest-property-taxes.

19. Morgan Scarborough, "Which Places Pay the Most Property Tax," Tax Foundation, 2015, https://taxfoundation.org/median-property-taxes-county-2011-2015/.

20. US Census, *American Community Survey 5-Year Estimates, Table DP03*, 2016, http://factfinder.census.gov.

21. Kate Stone Lombardi, "A Resource for the 'Other Westchester,'" *New York Times*, November 11, 2007, http://www.nytimes.com/2007/11/11/nyregion/nyregionspecial2/11col-we.html.

22. US Census, *American Community Survey 5-Year Estimates, Table DP02*, 2016, http://factfinder.census.gov.

23. US Census, American Community Survey, *Selected Characteristics of the Foreign-Born Population by Period of Entry into the United States: 2017 American Community Survey 1-Year Estimates*, https://factfinder.census.gov/bkmk/table/1.0/en/ACS/17_1YR/S0502/0500000US36119.

24. "26.8 Million Hispanics or Latinos in the US Labor Force in 2016," *TED: The Economics Daily* (Washington, DC: US Bureau of Labor Statistics, September 25, 2017), https://www.bls.gov/opub/ted/2017/26-point-8-million-hispanics-or-latinos-in-the-u-s-labor-force-in-2016.htm?view_full.

25. "26.8 Million Hispanics or Latinos."

26. Ben Gitis and Douglas H. Holtz-Eakin, "How Changes in Immigration Can Impact Future Worker Shortages in the United States and Silicon Valley," American Action Forum, October 23, 2015, accessed August 23, 2018, http://americanactionforum.org/research/how-changes-in-immigration-can-impact-future-worker-shortages-in-the-united.

27. Paul McDaniel, "Immigrants and Their Children Fill Gaps Left by Aging American Workforce," *American Immigration Council Immigration Impact,* June 20, 2013, accessed August 23, 2018, http://immigrationimpact.com/2013/06/20/immigrants-and-their-children-fill-gaps-left-by-aging-american-workforce/.

28. William Frey, *Diversity Explosion: How New Racial Demographics Are Remaking America* (Washington, DC: Brookings Institution Press, 2015).

29. US Department of Labor, "The 10 Fastest Growing Jobs," accessed August 27, 2018, https://blog.dol.gov/2015/03/15/the-10-fastest-growing-jobs.

30. Anthony Carnevale, Tamara Jayasundera, and Artem Gulish, *America's Divided Recovery: College Haves and Have-Nots* (Washington, DC: Georgetown University Center on Education and the Workforce, 2016), https://cew-7632.kxcdn.com/wp-content/uploads/Americas-Divided-Recovery-web.pdf.

31. *Connecting to Promising Careers: Middle-Skills Jobs in the Lower Hudson Valley, A Collaboration of Education, Business, and Government* (New York: JP Morgan Chase & Co., Westchester Community College, and NYC Labor Market Information Service, May 2016), http://www.sunywcc.edu/cms/wp-content/uploads/2016/05/PDF-1-Final-Report1.pdf.

32. Higher Education Opportunity Act of 2008, 20 U.S.C. § 1101a.

33. Vickie Choitz and Marcela Montes, *Working Together to Strengthen America's Immigrant Workforce: Partnerships between Community Colleges and Immigrant-Serving Organizations* (Washington, DC: The Aspen Institute, October 2016), accessed August 24, 2018, https://www.aspeninstitute.org/publications/working-together-strengthen-americas-immigrant-workforce-partnerships-community-colleges-immigrant-serving-organizations/.

34. Choitz and Montes, *Working Together.*

35. "In-State Tuition and Unauthorized Immigrant Students," National Conference of State Legislatures, February 19, 2014, accessed August 22, 2018, http://www.ncsl.org/research/immigration/in-state-tuition-and-unauthorized-immigrants.aspx.

36. "Dream Act of 2017: Summary and Answers to Frequently Asked Questions," National Immigration Law Center, accessed September 1, 2018, https://www.nilc.org/issues/immigration-reform-and-executive-actions/dream-act-2017-summary-and-faq.

37. Tom K. Wong, Sanaa Abrar, Tom Jawetz, Ignacia Rodriguez Kmec, Patrick O'Shea, Greisa Martinez Rosas, and Philip E. Wolgin, "Amid Legal and Political Uncertainty, DACA Remains More Important Than Ever," Center for American Progress, August 15, 2018, https://www.americanprogress.org/issues/immigration/news/2018/08/15/454731/amid-legal-political-uncertainty-daca-remains-important-ever.

38. Tom Jawetz, Nichole Prchal Svajlenka, and Philip E. Wolgin, "Dreams Deferred: A Look at DACA Renewals and Losses Post-March 5," Center for American Progress, March 2, 2018, https://www.americanprogress.org/issues/immigration/news/2018/03/02/447486/dreams-deferred-look-daca-renewals-losses-post-march-5/.

39. Bianca Quilantan, "Colleges Can't Completely Shield Undocumented Students if DACA Lapses: Here's What They Can Do," *Chronicle of Higher Education,* February 26, 2018, https://www.chronicle.com/article/Colleges-Can-t-Completely/242643.

40. For the latest updates on the DACA program, see https://www.nilc.org/issues/daca.

41. "Basic Facts about In-State Tuition for Undocumented Immigrant Students," National Immigration Law Center, last updated June 21, 2019, accessed September 1, 2018, https://www.nilc.org/issues/education/basic-facts-instate.

42. "Our Blue Ribbon Panel," Community College Consortium for Immigrant Education, accessed August 22, 2018, http://www.cccie.org/about/our-blue-ribbon-panel/.

43. "Leadership Profiles," Community College Consortium for Immigrant Education, accessed August 22, 2018, http://www.cccie.org/about/our-blue-ribbon-panel/leadership-profiles/.

44. Brian C. Rosenberg, "Speaking Out on Politics: When College Presidents Should Break 'Code of Silence,'" *The Washington Post,* October 5, 2015, https://www.washingtonpost.com/news/grade-point/wp/2015/10/05/speaking-out-on-politics-when-college-presidents-should-break-code-of-silence/?noredirect=on&utm_term=.d5645e5b52f7.

45. Travis Bradberry, "9 Things Emotionally Intelligent People Won't Do," *Forbes,* March 26, 2014, accessed August 23, 2018, https://www.forbes.com/sites/travisbradberry/2014/03/26/9-things-emotionally-intelligent-people-wont-do/#230cd0152d5e.

46. *Westchester Community College Diversity, Equity, and Inclusion Strategic Plan* (Valhalla, NY: Westchester Community College, 2017), http://www.sunywcc.edu/cms/wp-content/uploads/2017/09/Westchester-CC-DEI-Strategic-Plan.pdf.

47. Aleesia Forni, "County Creates Minority and Women Owned Businesses Task Force," *Westfair Communications,* August 15, 2018, accessed August 16, 2018, https://westfaironline.com/105770/county-creates-minority-and-women-owned-businesses-task-force/.

Chapter Two

Toward Equity

The Immigrant Experience at Miami Dade College

Malou C. Harrison

Perhaps no other conversation has challenged America's self-image more poignantly than the debate over immigration. "Patriotism," "human rights," "liberty," even "national security"—integral as they are to the truth of the American Dream—have become the linguistic elements of partisan discourse. Beyond the politics, however, the deeper questions remain—questions of the meaning of America in people's lives, and how this translates far and wide into the world.

Nearly sixty-six million people around the world have been forced from their homes, the highest levels of displacement on record, according to the United Nations High Commission on Refugees.[1] If our laws are slow to respond, it has everything to do with the dilemma that people at our doorstep pose. We are parochial and progressive in the same moment. Those who look, sing, dance, and worship differently test our boundaries. And they invite us to reengage with the basic questions that define our country—the land of the free, home of the brave.

THE CHANGING FACE OF AMERICA

The immigration debate is a continuing circumstance that has vacillated tremendously over time. Rhetoric about a "wall" coupled with more profoundly unfolding circumstances around separation and reunification of children and their emigrating families are the present order of the day. Given socioeconomic and political pushes and pulls of nations throughout the world, persons keep lining up to enter by any means possible, and likely will scale a fence or even stow away to plant their feet on American soil.

But just as surely as the face of this country is changing, it is equally certain that Congress must move swiftly to make an informed decision on comprehensive immigration reform. And what is the definition of *comprehensive*? Broad legislation would need to address demand for high- and low-skill labor; border security; legal status for undocumented residents; and enforcement, education, and social services in communities across the country.

Broad-based focus notwithstanding, clarity on our immigration policy would lend much-needed stability in an era of continual demographic change. In 1970, fewer than ten million immigrants lived in the United States. Today, immigrants account for 43 million people, 14 percent of the nation's 323 million. Immigrants and their US-born children equal about 27 percent of US inhabitants.[2]

Those numbers do not include approximately eleven million undocumented persons. More than half have lived here for ten years or more, and nearly one-third are the parents of US-born children.[3] Although enhanced border security remains the policy emphasis, individuals who arrived in the United States legally but overstayed their visas outnumber those who crossed the border illegally by six hundred thousand since 2007.[4] Customs and Border Protection data also show border crossings down 26 percent from 2017 to 2018, and arrests of suspected undocumented immigrants up by 40 percent.[5] Many apprehended at the border include Central American asylum seekers, who are often children fleeing violence in their countries. Among a host of other data and dire straits, these continue to stir the immigration debate; there appears to be little clarity on the horizon.

Deferred Action for Childhood Arrivals (DACA) remains critical to immigrant students and higher education institutions, particularly community colleges. In 2012, President Obama took action to offer renewable, two-year deportation deferrals and work permits to undocumented immigrants who had arrived in the United States as children. To date, eight hundred thousand DACA recipients have attended college, become employed, or served in the military.

The DACA program was rescinded in 2017, and at this writing Congress has not established legislation to ensure the status of those covered by DACA. A saving grace, though by no means a permanent solution, has been the federal court, which has ruled on several occasions that the program must remain open as long as legal challenges persist.

THE CHALLENGE OF POVERTY

Everyone in Miami has an immigrant story, and that includes me, a native of the island of Jamaica. At Miami Dade College (MDC), those stories bear fruit at graduation and the storytellers now power every facet of the local economy. They reflect the strengths and resilience immigrants have always brought to this country: grit and willingness to work hard, dedication to stand as a model for the next generation, pride in both their native country and their new homeland, plus courage to embrace hope and take risks toward a better life.

From countless immigrant success stories, MDC's cornerstone belief in the potential of each student is ever present. The college's open door reflects a serious and conscious commitment. But it was immigrants' vulnerabilities that helped, early on, to define the practical elements of student support. English language deficiencies, unfamiliarity with or the absence of family tradition in higher education, a need for personal attention and a supportive learning community, a lack of knowledge regarding societal and workforce expectations, healthcare needs, family dependency and basic skills development—all were and remain consistent issues for new arrivals. If these challenges seem familiar on an everyman or woman list of needs, it is because they belong to the broader, complex challenge of poverty, present at nearly every community college in the nation.

Beyond national origins, community college educators know that poverty is the generative—and generational—factor that most hinders student accomplishment. At MDC, 67 percent of students are classified as low income and 46 percent live beneath the federal poverty guideline.[6] Exit polls performed by the college on each departing student confirm financial need as the overwhelming reason that students drop out.

A range of additional factors completes the poverty context: 68 percent need at least one developmental course in basic skills for math, reading, writing, or English language. This challenge has been further complicated by state legislation that allows entering students to enroll in college-level courses regardless of skill level. The legislation also implies that colleges are prevented from assessing skill levels upon entry.

Sixty-two percent of MDC students attend part-time and 70 percent work while in school, with nearly 30 percent working at least thirty-five hours per week.[7] Those are hours lost for study and the essential campus connections with peers, faculty, and staff.

Lastly, 56 percent of MDC students are the first in their families to attend college. This one piece of data speaks to the profound effect of MDC and community colleges nationwide, altering the generational stranglehold of poverty. Unfortunately, the grip has eased only slightly. The Georgetown Center on Education and the Workforce reported that only a quarter of college freshmen born into the bottom half of the income distribution will earn a bachelor's degree by age twenty-four, while almost 90 percent of freshmen from families in the top income quartile will complete their degree.[8]

Ironically, such is the state of social mobility in the richest nation on earth. Economists from Harvard University and the University of California Berkeley found it to be no worse than it was in 1971. That is faint praise in the era of the "One Percent" and the historic breach between rich and poor,[9] with the highest levels of inequality since 1928.[10] Stagnant mobility places immigrants at an immediate disadvantage, and creates a generation of young people struggling to find stability in a radically new and overly dynamic workforce environment.

WELCOME TO MIAMI

Opened in 1960, just months after the first surge of Cuban arrivals, MDC offered a chance to start over. It quickly became the backbone of the region's evolving economic and civic environment.

Dade Junior College, South Florida's first public higher education institution, boasted an inaugural class of 1,428 students. The enrollment of seven black students also established the college as the first integrated junior college in Florida and the first integrated public college in the old Confederacy.[11] Fueled by the constant flow of new students from Cuba and an eager local population, the college grew faster than any other junior college in the nation. Enrollment reached 13,000 by 1964, and in 1967, with 23,000 students, Dade Junior became the largest college or university in Florida.[12] So just how did immigrants forge the character and values of the institution as well as influence the approach to student success?

The college's long-standing commitment to academic and student support was forged in these early years. MDC has grown to become a robust and innovative academic institution, offering an Honors College, baccalaureate degrees, and specialization across some three hundred major areas of study. But its early recognition of both the assets and vulnerabilities of immigrant students was crucial in the development of the college's character and values. The commitment has endured to address the ramifications of displacement, lack of family and community social capital as it pertains to higher education, and, perhaps most importantly, the effects of poverty.

Today, MDC is the largest public college or university in the nation, enrolling some 165,000 students at 8 campuses and several outreach centers. MDC's president, Dr. Eduardo J. Padrón, emigrated from Cuba in his midteens, and proudly lauds MDC as the alma mater that gave him his foundational start in life as a college student. President Padrón's own story as an immigrant reveals a remarkable "man for all seasons" immigrant experience and journey. His trajectory has been one of courage, selflessness, and a sense of purpose to transform the lives of others through the opportunity of education.

President Padrón recently added the eminent US Presidential Medal of Freedom to the roster of numerous, well-deserved national and international recognitions that have been bestowed on him. Because of his visionary leadership around equity, MDC's eight campuses and outreach centers continue to flourish as student-ready havens of education and training for immigrants.

One of MDC's locations is the Eduardo J. Padrón Campus, for which I serve as president, located in the heart of Miami's Little Havana neighborhood. Today, the Eduardo J. Padrón Campus offers students the full range of degree and short-term options and is the home campus for MDC's Dual Language Honors College; the signature Translation and Interpretation Studies program; a multi-optioned English program for nonnative English speakers; and the premier School of Education, which comprises teacher education in many subject areas including Teaching English to Speakers of Other Languages. But the Eduardo J. Padrón Campus began as a bilingual outreach center of MDC. By 1980, it was the largest bilingual facility in all of higher education, just in time to accommodate the latest wave of immigrants via the Mariel boatlift from Cuba.

The college's diversity has long been a defining characteristic. Today, students from 180 countries, speaking 90 languages, bring the world's cultures and viewpoints to its classrooms and campuses. Students of Hispanic origin make up more than 70 percent of the total enrollment, with students of Cuban heritage now joined by students with roots in all the countries in Central and South America. Among these and other students with international origins, 29 percent overall are non-US citizens. The remaining students are 17.6 percent African American and 7 percent white.

INTEGRATING IMMIGRANTS IN THE LARGER SUPPORT ENVIRONMENT AT MDC

MDC has implemented a variety of programs and strategies that target immigrant students' needs, which may overlap with the needs of other students. The college is intent on providing a supportive environment for all.

Learning English

The most obvious and overwhelming need of immigrants at MDC has always been to become adept in reading, understanding, writing, and speaking English. As evident as English proficiency is, it can become a discouragement to students who want to quickly advance academically. In an effort to effect balance between language progress and engagement in career learning, revisions have produced multiple tracks to address individual student needs. English-language education is anything but a one-size-fits-all proposition at MDC.

MDC's menu of options offers credit and noncredit English-language learning that includes English for academic purposes, English for speakers of other languages, and vocational English for speakers of other languages. Innovative variations exist within each program to help students accelerate their English-language learning, enroll concurrently in major coursework, and enable them to transition to the workforce without undue delays. Our college has been both strategic and responsive in ensuring a wide offering is available to address the diverse English-language acquisition needs of our students and the immigrant communities we serve.

Refugee/Entrant Vocational Education Services Training (REVEST)

Funded by the State of Florida Department of Children and Families Office of Refugee Services, the REVEST program was created in 1999 to serve the English language, adult basic education, and vocational training needs of adult refugees under the Cuban/Haitian Entrants Act.[13] The program also provides academic assessment, long-term advisement, referrals to other service agencies, transportation and childcare subsidies, and assistance with the translation and evaluation of foreign-earned credentials.

Because of Miami's geographic location in relation to the Caribbean islands, most participants in the program are from Cuba and Haiti. The program has served more than 60,000 clients to date. In academic year 2017–2018 alone, REVEST enrolled more than 4,500 students, whose origins are largely from Cuba, Haiti, and Venezuela. In this same period, REVEST issued some three thousand bus passes for students who needed help with public transportation.

Of students who enrolled in English-language training courses, 77 percent completed them successfully, and 86 percent of those taking vocational courses completed them successfully. More than three hundred students completed a full course of study in phlebotomy, private security, or information technology, affording them a direct entry into the workforce. Strong and active advocacy is badly needed for state and federal funding to continue to support REVEST and other high-impact immigrant support programs that show evidence of exemplary outcomes.

Road to Citizenship

MDC values its place as a beacon of hope for our local immigrant refugee community by not only providing needed training for employment and integration, but also ultimately facilitating a path to US citizenship. Citizenship classes are offered as a means of providing immigrant students and the larger community an opportunity to become familiarized with the US Citizenship and Immigration Services naturalization process. The sessions facilitate students' mastery of the knowledge and skills needed to be successful in the formal interview as well as in the associated English and civics tests. The offerings include:

1. Citizenship exam preparation is a month-long continuing education course that prepares students to take the US citizenship test while practicing English-language skills.

2. Terminology for the citizenship exam is a month-long class that covers the steps required to apply for naturalization and the topics covered in the citizenship exam.

3. Citizenship and civics classes are offered by the REVEST program for lawful permanent residents who reside in Miami-Dade County. The course provides students a certificate of completion.

Valuing Foreign-Trained Professionals

True to its responsive nature, in 2017 MDC reengineered its efforts of support and intervention toward a more structured and encompassing approach to serving the needs of foreign-trained professionals (FTP). Establishing the Office of FTP, appointing a dedicated director, and engaging internal and external constituents have proven fruitful in this regard. MDC's Office of FTP offers translation and evaluation of foreign transcripts and prior learning; academic and career advisement; and assistance with matriculation into English courses and certificate or degree programs that will expedite entry into workforce and licensure and credentialing.

In the 2017–2018 academic year, there were 280 career pathway meetings, sixty-one student evaluations and translations, and eleven scholarships awarded. We remain committed to the continuous improvement of our FTP program by evaluating our services and their efficacy with regard to number of students served, services rendered, and time frame for transition to work, whether or not students' transition was into the same or similar job sector.

Defending Our Dreamers

At MDC, we are proud of our legacy of empowerment with regard to Dreamers, as evidenced by our leadership and advocacy role as a founding partner of TheDream.US. A growing organization of some seventy-five partner colleges committed to serving and graduating Dreamers, TheDream.US offers a holistic array of wraparound services and support to undocumented youth. The organization's signature accomplishments have led to it being the nation's largest student success scholarship program for Dreamers, with more than $30 million having been awarded to support immigrant students.

Despite the United States being the only country a majority of Dreamers have ever known, they receive no federal assistance to pay for college, have limited access to state aid, and often face paying out-of-state tuition. MDC's eligible Dreamers have been proud recipients of much-needed financial assistance from TheDream.US, and our precollege and financial aid advisors are well equipped to facilitate the opportunity of these scholarships to our prospective students and those who are currently enrolled. MDC also offers in-state tuition waivers for DACA students. The tuition waivers may be renewed each term a student is registered at the college.

MDC'S STUDENT ACHIEVEMENT INITIATIVES (SAI) MODEL

Anyone who has ever been a tourist in New York City or any of the world's bustling metropolises has likely experienced the luxury of wandering. Not merely wandering, but doing so amid the multitudes hustling here and there, their invisible knowledge of how and where and what is driving everything, the rhythm and feel of the streets. When wandering, it's all fascinating—to tourists.

Immigrants, of course, have few luxuries upon arrival, least of all fascination at what they cannot understand. If they wander, they are likely lost and uncomfortable, hoping that a good Samaritan will appear—someone who will tell them the mysterious code of the how and where and what of everything.

Immigrants, although unique in their needs, are not entirely unlike the credulous throng of a new class of community college students. If we are realistic, however, immigrants and their classmates at community colleges face a more daunting collection of challenges. Grit and determination aside, they need a reliable roadmap and college mentor to help them navigate the journey.

MDC's SAI is the college's roadmap, its pioneering vision to scale support for each student, according to goals and needs, in successfully completing his or her personal college roadmap. It is the college's ambitious project to build a culture with specific policies, practices, and procedures that combat the many and deep-rooted challenges that students confront. The initiative depends on faculty, staff, administrators, and students working collaboratively, well beyond traditional norms and compartmentalization, to create an integrated approach to significantly improve student performance and completion outcomes.

Shark Path: MDC's Guided Pathway Model

Since 2013, cross-functional and cross-campus teams at MDC have designed and implemented strategies to ensure that students—including immigrant students—start off right, progress through programs of study, and earn their credentials. Shark Path, named for MDC's mascot, is a comprehensive and integrated pathway that aligns academic and student services to support student success at every stage of the journey.

The Shark Path initiative represents MDC's adaptation of the Guided Pathway model and, as such, represents an action plan developed between student and advisor that starts when students enter and guides them at each step of their academic journey, keeping them on an efficient path to completion. MDC's Shark Path collaborates with the Excelencia in Action (E-Action) network, where a select group of institutions and organizations benefit from the collective expertise and advocacy efforts of the network.[14] MDC's SAI model is central to its contribution to the goals of this collaborative.

Mandatory Shark Start Orientation

Between 2012 and 2019, more than sixty thousand first-time-in-college students will have participated in this orientation course. In 2017, "meta-major" orientations were held at all campuses to provide students with more information about career and educational options (including associate of arts versus associate of sciences transfer degree programs and stackable credentials) from workforce certificates to bachelor's degrees. These orientations also support the further scaling of math pathways.

At orientation, advisors offer recommended first-semester academic plans and discuss programs of study and course choices during individual sessions with students. First-semester plans include mathematics, English, an introductory course in the chosen program of study, an elective, and a first-year experience (FYE) course that helps to demystify the college culture and expectations and provides support in study skills and time and stress management. The FYE course is particularly valuable for immigrant students, and is mandatory for all associate degree–seeking students and those in developmental courses.

COMMUNITY PARTNERSHIPS FOR
PRECOLLEGE PREPARATION

For immigrants and many low-income families, much remains mysterious and intimidating about the universe of higher education. MDC, with funding from the Lumina Foundation, embarked on the HACER initiative in 2013. HACER stands for Hispanic Access to College Education Resources and is also the Spanish word for "to do." In Miami-Dade County, there is much "to do" to address Hispanics' historical deficits in college success. Approximately 60 percent of Hispanics in the county have completed high school, and just 38 percent have achieved a postsecondary degree.[15]

Working closely with Miami-Dade County public schools, the local state university, and a full range of nonprofit and business partners, MDC reached into the community to help both newly arrived and long-standing residents upgrade their awareness of the possibility of gaining a college education. Overall, nineteen organizations across key sectors of the community collaborated to ensure that more students graduated from high school and completed their college educations at MDC and its partner state university. Community-based organizations, Hispanic-serving organizations, and corporations including Bank of America, Greater Miami and South Florida Hispanic Chambers of Commerce, Univision, and more stepped forward in support of HACER initiatives.

Those initiatives, which have been sustained at MDC beyond the completion of HACER, include financial aid literacy workshops; Free Application for Federal Student Aid (FAFSA) marathon sessions that assist students and parents to complete and submit the FAFSA form; and teacher collaboration/professional development projects, training high school content-area teachers in math, reading, and writing to strengthen articulation. Much HACER activity contributed to the ongoing development of the Completion by Design initiative, a five-year project (2011–2016) funded by the Bill and Melinda Gates Foundation that equipped community colleges to guide students toward graduation, credential transfer, and, ultimately, meaningful work. MDC was one of nine colleges in three states (Florida, North Carolina, and Ohio) that participated in this initiative.[16]

LESSONS LEARNED

The work of MDC in developing the SAI model is an effort to reach beyond the demographics and accumulated data. The faculty and staff who make the initiative tick, in a highly structured and strategic fashion, are really aiming for the heart of motivation in students. It has often been said that MDC's ultimate goal with students, regardless of discipline or degree, is to graduate students who have turned on to learning and discovered the learner within themselves—even fallen in love with learning.

As simple as that sounds, this is a profound and challenging rediscovery. Learning and creativity are often the work of undoing: shedding the layers of attitude and doubt that our students bring to campus. Too often, students harbor limits—stories they tell themselves that must give way to new stories of possibility and achievement, of knowing themselves and their gifts in ways that their history would not allow.

In 2014, a *New York Times Magazine* article, "Who Gets to Graduate," chronicled the work of education researchers at Stanford University.[17] They began from a point of view familiar to MDC faculty and staff: students fell short of their potential due to the presence of doubts about their ability. Further, they found these feelings to be especially virulent at transition points that included the first year of college. Such feelings were expressly problematic among students who might view themselves as having something to prove, which certainly includes immigrant students in a new cultural environment.

Two primary stumbling blocks emerged: doubts about whether they could ever truly belong at their institution, and misgivings about their intelligence. The researcher Carol Dweck identified an entity theory of knowledge that had ensnared too many vulnerable students. In the stories they told themselves, they simply weren't smart enough. They had a fixed quantity of intelligence that wouldn't budge no matter how hard they studied.

Although it may sound simplistic, MDC is helping students undo the old false stories that lower expectations and set the stage for failure and recurring poverty. Instead, strategically and by design, step by small step, MDC encourages students to entertain new stories about themselves, and then supports them in learning how to sustain the results.

For MDC, the proud host to immigrants in their education, training, and aspirational endeavors, student success demands an embrace of the whole student. Our institution's commitment to equity in education for immigrants is unwavering. Quoting MDC's president, Dr. Eduardo J. Padrón, "Our immigrant communities represent the best of our nation's values and beliefs. They are examples to all of the importance of hard work, dedication, and perseverance, and it is imperative that they are supported and motivated to achieve success in every aspect of their lives."

The formula, as espoused by our college, is simple yet demanding: rigorous standards, high expectations, a comprehensive and intrusive support environment, and experiential opportunities. I wholeheartedly embrace the old adage, "It takes a village." Certainly, our college remains committed to continuing to be a dynamic convener and partner with public- and private-sector stakeholders toward strengthening immigrant equity. America will only continue to grow and prosper in its domestic prowess and global competitiveness if we create a level playing field of educational and socioeconomic support and opportunities for immigrants, backed by appropriate immigration legislation.

NOTES

1. United Nations High Commission on Refugees, *Figures at a Glance, Statistical Yearbooks*, accessed August 16, 2018, http://www.unhcr.org/en-us/figures-at-a-glance.html.

2. Council on Foreign Relations, *The US Immigration Debate*, last modified July 2, 2018, https://www.cfr.org/backgrounder/us-immigration-debate-0.

3. Drew DeSilver, "US Income Inequality, on Rise for Decades, Is Now Highest since 1928," The Pew Research Center, last modified December 5, 2013, http://www.pewresearch.org/fact-tank/2013/12/05/u-s-income-inequality-on-rise-for-decades-is-now-highest-since-1928/.

4. Center for Migration Studies, "The 2,000 Mile Wall in Search of a Purpose: Since 2007 Visa Overstays Have Outnumbered Undocumented Border Crossers by a Half Million," *Journal on Migration and Human Security* (2017): 124–36, http://cmsny.org/publications/jmhs-visa-overstays-border-wall/.

5. Center for Migration Studies, "The 2,000 Mile Wall."

6. Miami Dade College, *Institutional Research, Fact Book*, accessed August 16, 2018, http://www.mdc.edu/ir/Fact%20Book/MDC%20Highlights%20and%20Facts_Nov2014rvd.pdf.

7. Miami Dade College, *Institutional Research, Fact Book*.

8. Anthony Carnevale and Jeff Strohl, *Rewarding Strivers* (New York: The Century Foundation, 2010).

9. Raj Chetty, Nathaniel Hendren, Patrick Kline, and Emmanuel Saez, "Where Is the Land of Opportunity? The Geography of Intergenerational Mobility in the United States," *Quarterly Journal of Economics* 129, no. 4 (2014): 1553–623.

10. DeSilver, "US Income Inequality."

11. Miami Dade College, *Under Construction: Twenty-Five Years of Miami-Dade Community College 1960–1985* (Miami: Lion & Thorne, 1988).

12. Miami Dade College, *Under Construction*.

13. Adult and Community Educators of Florida, *REVEST Program*, accessed August 12, 2018, https://aceofflorida.org/.

14. Excelencia in Education, *Programs for Latino Student Success*, accessed August 18, 2018, https://www.edexcelencia.org/programs-latino-student-success.

15. US Census Bureau, *Quick Facts: Miami-Dade County, Florida*, accessed August 16, 2018, https://www.census.gov/quickfacts/fact/table/miamidadecountyflorida/POP060210.

16. Bill and Melinda Gates Foundation, *Completion by Design*, accessed August 12, 2018, https://www.completionbydesign.org/s/.

17. Paul Tough, "Who Gets to Graduate," *New York Times Magazine*, May 15, 2014, https://www.nytimes.com/2014/05/18/magazine/who-gets-to-graduate.html.

Chapter Three

Taking the Support of Immigrant Students to New Heights

Gail O. Mellow

The Trump administration's efforts to dramatically overhaul America's immigration laws and practices struck at the very core of LaGuardia Community College. LaGuardia has a nearly fifty-year history of welcoming, educating, and graduating students from outside the United States; more than 60 percent of our students are foreign-born. At our campus located in Queens, New York, the single most diverse county in the nation, we educate one of the most diverse groups of students in the United States. While our commitment to our students, their families, and our neighbors has remained unwavering, ensuring their safety and well-being has presented heightened challenges in the changed and uncertain immigration, travel, and law enforcement landscape that now surrounds us.

This chapter describes the practical steps LaGuardia has taken to respond to the current immigration rhetoric and realities, by amplifying and reaffirming our commitment to diversity, justice, and inclusion. Our efforts have been practical and wide reaching: ensuring that every member of the campus community is aware of and fully understands the unique needs of our immigrant students, and that we can mobilize campus and community resources to provide immediate emergency support when student needs arise.

Stepping up our commitment to immigrants has had lasting benefits, enabling us to be a beacon of civility for all members of our campus community. Although LaGuardia has a uniquely diverse immigrant student body, our lessons learned are replicable for other colleges seeking to operationalize a campus-wide response to threats to student well-being.

A UNIQUE STUDENT POPULATION AND
CAMPUS COMMUNITY

Since its founding in 1971, LaGuardia has always opened its doors of higher education to all. Our mission embodies the uniqueness and dreams of our students and the needs of our world: to educate and graduate one of the most diverse student populations in the country to become critical thinkers and socially responsible citizens who help to shape a rapidly evolving society.

The doors to our campus are open wide. LaGuardia welcomes all students; an open admission policy permits enrollment by any student who is a high school graduate or has earned a high school equivalency diploma. We also offer alternative pathways for students seeking to earn a high school equivalency diploma. Each year, more than 45,000 students from more than 150 countries, speaking 96 languages, come to LaGuardia. Even students who lack legal immigration status qualify for enrollment.

Undocumented students are generally ineligible for state or federal financial aid, but they do benefit from a 2001 New York State law that allows them to pay in-state tuition if they meet certain residency and educational requirements. Additionally, in January 2019, New York State passed the Dream Act, which for the first time offers eligible undocumented students access to state financial aid and scholarships for higher education. As a public institution within the City University of New York (CUNY) system, the largest urban university system in the United States, we have an open campus; our facilities are open to members of the public, who may come and go freely upon showing valid identification.

In the weeks following the 2016 presidential election, there was understandably heightened concern across campus about our continued ability to protect and serve the immigrant, international, and undocumented members of our community. Of particular concern was the fate of our Deferred Action for Childhood Arrival (DACA) students: those who had taken advantage of the 2012 immigration policy announced by then-President Obama and had been given temporary permission to stay in the United States. Under DACA, hundreds of LaGuardia students brought to the United States without sufficient documentation as children received a renewable two-year period of deferred action from deportation by the US Department of Homeland Security, as well as eligibility for an employment authorization document, giving them permission to work legally.

Having provided confidential information in their applications—from fingerprints to street addresses and cell phone numbers—there was, and remains, tremendous uncertainty as to the safety of DACA recipients' information and whether it will be shared with Immigration and Customs Enforcement (ICE) in support of deportation proceedings. There were also more general fears about immigration and other law enforcement officials coming on campus to seize records or arrest or detain students. Although a 2011 ICE policy memorandum was meant to ensure that enforcement actions by ICE officers and agents did not take place at sensitive locations such as schools and places of worship, there were legitimate fears and a great deal of uncertainty about the future of the nation's immigration laws under the Trump administration.

As 2016 ended, I joined with hundreds of other higher education leaders issuing statements of support for undocumented students and urging the president-elect not to rescind DACA. Closer to campus, I was determined that, before Inauguration Day in January 2017, LaGuardia would have in place specific, concrete steps to make sure that our students, faculty, and staff could obtain legal assistance, financial help, access to benefits, and other supports.

I also wanted to ensure that we were prepared to respond forcefully to any incidents of harassment and intimidation, either on or off our campus. Beyond recognizing the need for enhanced understanding of the complex legal environment in our legal and public safety departments, we mobilized expertise and resources in areas such as marketing and communications, student affairs, and government and community relations. Wanting input from and engagement of as many faculty, staff, and students as possible, I appointed a campus-wide ad-hoc group to help craft our action agenda for the new year.

THE CALL TO ACTION: MOBILIZING ACROSS THE CAMPUS AND COMMUNITY

Reflecting their commitment to stand and act together, the ad-hoc group began meeting weekly as the LaGuardia Rising Committee. Interest in the committee's work spread rapidly, with membership more than doubling as 2017 unfolded. Coming together weekly enabled the committee to surface and respond quickly to emerging needs. Other important benefits were the ability to address rumors and to provide emotional support to students and to colleagues, particularly during times of fast-moving policy changes.

The committee's initial recommendations to me focused on four priorities: increasing campus-wide awareness and understanding of relevant laws and law enforcement practices, troubleshooting and improving our student record-keeping practices, increasing student awareness of the resources available to support them and their families, and improving student access to lawyers.

In my original charge to the committee, I explicitly tasked them with compiling and analyzing all applicable laws. For their recommendations to be actionable, committee members needed to have a deeper understanding of the myriad federal, state, and city immigration and law enforcement practices that pertain to current immigrants, undocumented students, and holders of different types of visas. Perhaps the most urgent legal landscape to navigate was understanding the practices and priorities of the LaGuardia public safety department; of particular concern was the fear that students might be detained by ICE and removed from the campus.

The committee spent considerable time becoming better informed about campus public safety practices. They learned that public safety has a close working relationship with the New York City Police Department, Federal Bureau of Investigation, and other critical law enforcement agencies. Barring an active emergency, in order to arrest a student, external law enforcement officers would have to present a valid search warrant. Even in those circumstances, public safety would locate the student and accompany them to a discrete location where the arrest would take place. More generally, in the course of their routine activities on campus, public safety's practices are not to inquire about immigration status and, consistent with CUNY-wide policy, our staff would take no action to assist in the enforcement of immigration laws except as required by law.

Hearing firsthand from the college's senior lawyers and public safety officials helped the committee distinguish rhetoric from realities about what could and was actually taking place on the LaGuardia campus. We as a community had provided, and would continue to provide, as safe and welcoming an environment as legally possible. Committee members felt strongly that the entire campus community would benefit from hearing how strong, effective, and thoughtful our public safety department's practices and personnel were. At their urging, we featured these and other campus immigration-related practices and resources at a panel discussion at LaGuardia's opening faculty and staff meeting in March 2017.

Another priority recommendation was related to the treatment of and access to information about select students' immigration status. As noted previously, New York State allows an undocumented or out-of-status student to pay in-state tuition, provided they meet certain requirements, including filing an affidavit stating that they will apply to legalize their status as soon as they are eligible. Committee members discovered that university record-keeping procedures required that student recipients of in-state tuition be labeled "UNDOCUMENTED" and that, inadvertently, this information field was widely accessible to faculty and staff, well beyond the limited number of key financial services staff who needed access to this data point to oversee such students' financial status. One of the committee's early accomplishments was surfacing this situation, which, when brought to the attention of CUNY's central office, was promptly rectified across all of its campuses. A much more restrictive access policy was put in place, dramatically reducing the number of staff who would have access to this information going forward.

Resource constraints are a reality for most LaGuardia students, more than 70 percent of whom have an annual family income under $30,000. We wanted to be sure we were doing all that we could to support the financial needs of immigrant students, and that they were aware of and felt they could access support safely and confidentially. One of the committee's most lasting and significant contributions came about from its undertaking an inventory of resources available on campus, through CUNY or elsewhere in the community, to support undocumented and other immigrant students and their families with legal, financial, emotional, or housing and food security issues.

Although the completed inventory revealed there were extensive resources, it also clearly illustrated that this information was literally all over the place. Because information related to immigrant matters was not in a centralized location, it was not easily accessible. Nor was there any way to communicate effectively with students most in need of that information, particularly about urgent matters such as looming filing deadlines or travel restrictions.

Two immediate steps we took were to create a new online resource webpage clearly labeled "Immigrant Support." If a student needs immediate confidential legal or financial help, or is worried about his or her own or a family member's immigration status or the ability to stay in school, resources and services are now listed succinctly. In addition to creating this "go-to" digital resource, contact information was provided for a senior student affairs professional who is available 24/7, regardless of the student's immigration status, for help locating appropriate resources. The Immigrant Support webpage continues to receive thousands of hits monthly.

Anticipating increased demand for legal services, committee members evaluated the availability and nature of legal services available to students on or off our campus, as well as awareness of such services. They learned that, although different programs brought pro bono lawyers on campus, students reported long waits for appointments, and few lawyers had immigration experience, particularly in nuanced areas such as advising DACA students on their legal options.

Ironically, committee members discovered that they had overlapping relationships with various external organizations such as the Legal Aid Society and Catholic Charities of New York, but had not previously thought to coordinate the college's outreach efforts. By working collaboratively, they have been able to improve dramatically the number and skills of lawyers now coming on campus to meet with students. A community outreach manager in the college's external affairs division is now centrally coordinating outreach activities to these organizations as well as to other immigrant support and advocacy organizations.

The committee's final recommendation, which I accepted, was a request to continue to serve on an ongoing basis as an advisory and coordinating body. Having a centralized coordinating structure to help disseminate information rapidly turned out to be quite timely, when a mere seven days after his inauguration, President Trump announced the first of several travel bans, barring citizens from seven Muslim-majority countries from entering the United States for 90 days and all refugees for 120 days. The ongoing court battles over the travel bans, as well as the ongoing uncertainty and complicated status of the DACA program, have provided the committee with new, persistent challenges.

ENSURING A COORDINATED RESPONSE ACROSS THE CAMPUS AND THE COMMUNITY

The real and threatened changes to the treatment of recent immigrants, international students, and other individuals who lack legal immigration status have been a call to action for the entire LaGuardia Community College community. Whether it is monitoring the seemingly endless court and legislative developments pertaining to the travel bans or the DACA program, or helping a member of our community with an immediate need for support, we now have a truly campus-wide capacity to act. We have upped our game in ensuring that when there is breaking news or immigration-related policy changes, we are able to respond in a timely, coordinated, and thoughtful manner.

LaGuardia serves a uniquely diverse and immigrant-rich student body, but the lessons we have learned about improving our capacity to mobilize immigrant supports are replicable to higher education and other institutions seeking to improve their support of immigrants.

In a time of heightened anxiety and confusion surrounding breaking news that affects members of the campus community, it is imperative that leaders be out in front and offer frequent, visible assurances that their institution is on top of the developments and mobilizing an appropriate campus response. A key resource is the ability to disseminate accurate information in a timely manner to affected audiences. Having networks and structures in place both to analyze and vet information is essential, particularly in highly nuanced areas such as immigration law.

In this regard, LaGuardia has benefited from its relationships with external partners in state and local government, including New York State Governor Andrew M. Cuomo's Office of New Americans, and New York City Mayor Bill de Blasio's Office of Immigrant Affairs. We have also worked closely with community-based organizations such as the New York Immigration Coalition, Catholic Migration Services, and the Legal Aid Society, to connect our students with reliable information and expert advice.

Particularly in academic institutions, where different ideas and perspectives are acknowledged and debated with vigor, it is essential that every member of the institution be aware of students' as well as their own rights and responsibilities. One of those responsibilities that we have worked hard to reinforce is the need for all members of the campus community to be aware of the resources we have on campus and in our local community to provide immediate, emergency support whenever any student needs that support. Some of the ways in which we have raised awareness of these resources have included providing "know your rights" trainings, hosting immigrant information resource fairs, and providing briefings on committee developments to various internal groups such as our college senate and faculty departments.

Beyond just our legal, public safety, and student affairs staff, our faculty, frontline staff, and administrators are now better equipped to help any student or colleague find their way to assistance. The committee continues to be a go-to resource, where any member of the LaGuardia community can present concerns about how the institution is supporting immigrants and help construct appropriate institutional responses to emerging needs.

LOOKING BACK AND MOVING FORWARD

Every single day, students from across the globe come to LaGuardia to learn, to become inspired, and to realize their dreams for a better life for themselves and their families. Our work at LaGuardia is more vital now than ever before. Although the past year has brought announcements and headlines that contradict all we believe in at the college, I am proud of how our campus community has stood together and redoubled our commitment to the values of inclusiveness and openness. Faced with unprecedented uncertainty about the ability of too many of our students and their family members to stay in the United States, we have faced down the heartache and doubts with that which we can be certain about: our own values and the critical mission we serve.

Chapter Four

The CEO's Role in Building Education Pathways for All Aspiring Americans

Lee D. Lambert

My family and I settled in the Olympia, Washington, area in the summer of 1977 after spending three years in Seoul, South Korea. My father, a US Army veteran who was born and raised in North Carolina, and my mother, born and raised in South Korea, had decided to relocate to the United States. It was not uncommon during my Olympia high school years to be asked by my classmates, "Where are you from?"

"America," I always replied.

"You can't be from America. Where were you born?"

"I was born in Seoul, South Korea."

My response rarely satisfied my teen interlocutors, who had difficulty reconciling my nationality with my appearance. These conversations stay with me to this day, and I share this personal narrative because it inspires me, as CEO of Pima Community College (PCC), located in Tucson, Arizona, to ensure that PCC enables all our students, *wherever they live or have lived*, to have the opportunity to pursue their personal vision of the American Dream through the promise inherent in higher education.

THE LANDSCAPE

Each year, PCC provides some 42,000 credit and noncredit students with education and training in dozens of programs leading either to direct employment or to transfer into a four-year college or university. Our adult education program helps thousands of our Pima County neighbors take the critical first step on their education journey, and our rising workforce development division meets the needs of local employers and industry. In sum, we supply the education resources for our town's residents, be they Americans (born or naturalized), refugees, immigrants, or from another country.

Many in our refugee and immigrant communities face formidable hurdles when they arrive in the United States. Some refugees and immigrants come to Tucson speaking very little English. Some may have little, if any, formal education. Additionally, there are cultural barriers to overcome. However, community colleges such as PCC do their best to provide programs and services to support the success of our refugee and immigrant communities while facing multiple complex challenges.

Like many community colleges, PCC's enrollment has fallen. Our full-time student equivalency in 2017 is lower than it was 1992. In 1980, Arizona voters passed an expenditure limitation law that links spending of public funds by institutions like PCC to our enrollment. Since 2015, the state of Arizona has zeroed out appropriations to PCC and to the state's largest community college district, the Maricopa Community College District in metropolitan Phoenix.

PCC has chosen not to recoup those lost funds by increasing tuition. We are committed to keeping tuition low, in recognition of the modest circumstances of many of our students. In 2019, the PCC governing board raised tuition by $2 per credit hour to $84.50 for in-state residents. Our other major source of revenue is property taxes. PCC can ask for a maximum 2 percent increase in the county property tax rate from a public that increasingly, and rightfully, scrutinizes our expenditures.

Communities like Pima County are experiencing competition from institutions both down the street and across the country. Online and competency-based models are fueling a stealth enrollment drain, as individuals can stay local and attend a college or university hundreds, if not thousands, of miles away without having to leave the comfort of their chosen community. Looking ahead, shifting demographics will have significant implications for higher education. Carleton College economist Nathan Grawe puts it well in his 2017 book, *Demographics and the Demand for Higher Education*. Grawe argues that the Great Recession of 2008–2009 brought about a "birth dearth,"[1] a steep decline in the birth rate. Additionally, the foreign-born population in the United States is almost forty-four million, or 13.5 percent of the total US population,[2] and growing. About one in four (23 percent) of all US college students are immigrants or the children of immigrants.[3]

In Arizona, a lower percentage of twenty-five-and-older foreign-born (18.2 percent) than native-born (27.2 percent) individuals has a bachelor's degree or higher.[4] Grawe concludes, "There is no argument: demographic change is reshaping the population of the United States in ways that raise challenges for higher education. Through immigration, interstate migration, and fertility differences across demographic groups, the country's population is tilting toward the Southwest in general and the Hispanic Southwest in particular."[5] A community college CEO in Arizona, or anywhere, would be remiss if her institution did not explore initiatives to engage the foreign-born, whether refugee, immigrant, or an international student, in order to ameliorate enrollment challenges.

Community college leaders also must understand and leverage local culture regarding immigrant and refugee education. As our nation struggles with issues surrounding immigration, the city of Tucson has been clear about its commitment to all its residents, be they American-born or naturalized, refugee or immigrant. Since the Tucson city council's passage of resolution 21944 in 2012,[6] Tucson has been an official "immigrant welcoming city," in recognition that "our city's identity is built upon its promise of equality, esteem for diversity, and commitment to innovation." And it should be noted that Tucson, thanks to the work of a Presbyterian church on the city's predominantly Hispanic South Side, is commonly recognized as the birthplace of the sanctuary movement.[7] We must be mindful of our community's commitments, heritage, and culture.

DREAMERS

Society's support for refugees and immigrants can wax or wane, and Arizona is a perfect example of this dynamic. In February 2013, the PCC governing board approved in-state resident tuition for students with Deferred Action for Childhood Arrivals (DACA) status. Unfortunately, the Arizona Supreme Court ruled in April 2018 that existing state law does not allow the granting of in-state resident tuition benefits to DACA recipients. (It should be noted that in 2017, PCC filed an amicus curiae brief supporting the Maricopa Community College District's opposition to a lower-court ruling prohibiting charging DACA students in-state resident tuition.) As a result of the court's decision, the college is preparing a tuition schedule to take effect beginning with the fall 2018 semester that will charge DACA students out-of-state nonresident tuition.

DACA students, often brought to the United States at a very young age by their parents, are bright and articulate, and are among the most talented students we graduate each year. The Arizona Supreme Court's decision and other decisions and activities at the national level have created an environment of uncertainty among DACA students. Naturally, they are scared about losing access to their education.

PCC has responded with consistent messages of solidarity, whether in an email telling students to "breathe," or in a face-to-face meeting with college leadership. In the spring of 2018, I met with some of these students to share my support of their success. I let them know we are looking at all legally available options for them to continue their education, and are examining ways we can creatively leverage partnerships to possibly provide some financial relief. We are working with Student Affairs—our advisors, counselors, and financial aid staffers—to ensure that DACA students get consistent, accurate information about the 2018–2019 tuition changes; are directed to scholarship resources, such as the PCC Foundation, that provide grants and financial assistance to students regardless of their immigration status; and are treated with compassion and empathy. That said, the reality is that PCC, like all institutions, must uphold the law.

REDEFINING "COMMUNITY"

Pima Community College supports a broad view of what constitutes a community. First and foremost, through its open-access provisions, the PCC governing board's mission fulfillment framework[8] expressly directs the college to aid all those who pass through its doors: "College Mission: PCC is an open-admissions institution providing affordable, comprehensive educational opportunities that support student success and meet the diverse needs of its students and community." Among our college's values are open admissions and open access: "We value open admissions and access to our programs and services for all who may benefit from them, regardless of where they are starting from or what their final goal may be." The college's institutional "north star" comprises student success, community engagement, and diversity.

The power of policy cannot be discounted. Policy is institutional commitment, and resources flow from policy. For example, the diversity policy of the Pima County Community College District's governing board commits the college "to providing and supporting programs, services, and training that will enable all students . . . to achieve their educational and career objectives"[9] and has given rise to a PCC initiative to create an Immigrant and Refugee Resource Center that will help these populations successfully navigate life in their new country.

Given these policies and directions, as CEO I am compelled to advance immigrant and refugee education by embedding diversity, equity, and inclusion into college processes, infrastructure, and budget; by creating high-level community connections; and by advocating the economic and social-justice imperatives driving PCC immigrant and refugee education activities, such as through the signing the Community College Consortium for Immigrant Education's Presidents for New American Success Pledge.[10]

REFUGEE EDUCATION PROGRAM

Few programs at PCC embody a commitment to aspiring Americans more effectively than the Refugee Education Program (REP). And the reality is that few programs are needed more. Since 1980, more than seventy thousand refugees, speaking more than forty languages, have resettled in Arizona.[11] In fiscal year 2018, Arizona was the sixth-highest destination in the nation for refugees.[12] In Tucson, 1,148 refugees were resettled in fiscal year 2016 and 964 in fiscal year 2017.[13] That number fell to 132 in the first three months of 2018, following the federal government's decision to prohibit citizens of Somalia, Sudan, and Syria—which had been the second, third, and fourth most common countries of origin for Tucson refugees—from entering the United States. The Democratic Republic of Congo, Burundi, Pakistan, Eritrea, and Afghanistan now constitute the top countries of origin of refugees to Tucson.[14] The need remains acute.

The REP has been an English-language training contractor for the State of Arizona Refugee Resettlement Program since 1978. The REP works in conjunction with the other Refugee Resettlement Program contractors to provide immediate workplace and survival English for all new adult refugee arrivals. The city is home to numerous organizations helping aspiring Americans: the local chapters of national networks such as the International Rescue Committee, Lutheran Social Services, and Catholic Community Services are designated refugee resettlement agencies.

The program is dynamic and flexible, as it must quickly retrain its faculty and staff to meet the constantly changing profiles of incoming refugees' English, literacy, and educational backgrounds. Thus, it succeeds on many levels. Thanks to excellent coordination with employers of refugees, REP classes respond to employer and student needs, and to resettlement agency case management and job developers. The result is that newly arrived refugees have a job placement rate of 87 percent to 90 percent between the first sixty and ninety days after arrival. That same coordination allows refugees easy reentry into PCC's Adult Basic Education for College and Career programs as well as PCC certificate and degree programs, once individuals and families have established time and space for further study and credentialing.

Recently, the biggest challenge the program has faced is scaling activities to meet increased community interest. In late fall 2016, the Pima County community showed an outpouring of support for refugees. Volunteer coordinators of area resettlement agencies and refugee service providers scrambled to find placements and build training capacity for community members who wanted to get involved. The REP responded to each challenge by hosting the first of many community-wide "Refugee 101s": community members could go to a different location each month to learn about the process of resettlement, meet representatives from service providers, and learn more about volunteer opportunities available in the community.

The REP also partnered with a community literacy organization to rework a volunteer English-tutor training for both agency volunteers and community members who volunteer on their own to work with refugee second-language adult emergent readers. These are individuals who are learning print literacy for the first time as well as the English language. In eleven months, 342 community members attended the Refugee 101 workshop, and 106 individuals received in-depth training to work with second-language adult emergent readers.

More broadly speaking, one of the key lessons learned in serving immigrant and refugee students over the past several years has been an understanding of the importance of a well-informed and culturally sensitive coordinated community response network. Ideally, in such a network all referrals would be "warm handoffs"—that is, they would be conducted in person with the refugee and members of the relevant organizations present, so that the refugee receives a consistent message regarding access to employment and educational services. PCC strives for that degree of customer service for our native students, and our refugee clients deserve nothing less.

LESSONS LEARNED

For a community college leader in the United States of America in 2018, simply sharing accurate information in context has become increasingly necessary. Data that places education for refugee, immigrant, and international students in perspective is especially important because failing to serve these populations will be costly to individual higher education institutions and to the US economy. A 2017 Brookings Institution analysis[15] estimates that educating foreign students brings in at least $35 billion to the US economy. This makes education one of our nation's leading exports, with "exactly the same economic effects as when we sell soybeans or coal abroad."

The reality is that the potential cost to US economic development is immeasurable. Remember that many who come to the United States are here for the rest of their lives, as they likely cannot return to their home nation. Immigrants play an outsized role as entrepreneurs and as founders of major American companies. Almost half of the companies in the 2017 Fortune 500 were founded or cofounded by immigrants or their children.[16] Jerry Yang was a student from Taiwan who graduated from Stanford and founded Yahoo! Andy Grove arrived from Hungary, graduated from the University of California–Berkeley, and co-founded Intel Corp. Who will follow in their footsteps and create the Next Big Thing on the soil of their adopted nation? That is an unknown, but is pleasant to contemplate. What is increasingly clear is that, given reasoned examination, providing a welcoming learning environment for refugee, immigrant, and international students can power entrepreneurship and economic development. It is a venture that any American should support.

PERSONAL REFLECTION

Allow me to conclude with a return to my days growing up in Olympia. Because I had the good fortune of having an American father, who was stationed overseas as a soldier in the Army, as a child I was able to enter the United States as a citizen, and went on to take advantage of the myriad opportunities that come with citizenship. Since 2013, I have been the chancellor of PCC.

Contrast my experience with that of another foreign-born individual, also brought to the United States as a young child. She was brought by undocumented parents who were born in Mexico and came to the United States seeking something better. The child excelled in Tucson's public schools and, upon graduation from high school, she chose PCC to continue her education, in no small part because PCC offered students like her in-state resident tuition, at least until the Arizona Supreme Court's decision in April 2018. As of this writing she has calculated that, with her current financial resources, she cannot afford to attend PCC full-time. She has enough money to take one class per semester. In short, her dreams have been put on hold.

What is the difference between these two individuals, both foreign-born? Both grew up within the borders of the same United States of America, a nation built on equality of opportunity. Although Americans should honor and celebrate their heritage, the circumstances surrounding their birth, specifically where their parents were born, should not determine their destiny, any more than the zip codes in which they were brought up. Those who seek to divide, to allot or withhold education based on accidents of birth, must be opposed. In my view, and in service to all aspiring Americans, it is imperative that education break through the walls that divide us and be a bulwark that fortifies social equity in our great, diverse society.

NOTES

1. Jeffrey R. Young, "A Slow-Moving Storm: Why Demographic Changes Mean Tough Challenges for College Leaders," *EdSurge*, April 17, 2018, https://www.edsurge.com/news/2018-04-17-a-slow-moving-storm-why-demographic-changes-mean-tough-challenges-for-college-leaders.

2. Jie Zong, Jeanne Batalova, and Jeffrey Hallock, "Frequently Requested Statistics on Immigrants and Immigration in the United States," Migration Policy Institute, February 8, 2018, US Census Bureau, 2016 American Community Survey, https://

www.migrationpolicy.org/article/frequently-requested-statistics-immigrants-and-immigration-united-states.

3. Sandra Staklis and Laura Horn, *New Americans in Postsecondary Education: A Profile of Immigrant and Second-Generation American Undergraduates* (Washington, DC: National Center for Education Statistics, 2012), 4.

4. US Census Bureau, American Community Survey, 2009, accessed August 1, 2018, https://www.census.gov/prod/2012pubs/p20-566.pdf.

5. Nathan Grawe, *Demographics and the Demand for Higher Education* (Baltimore: Johns Hopkins University Press, 2017), 2.

6. "Tucson: An Immigrant Welcoming City," City of Tucson, accessed May 1, 2018, https://www.tucsonaz.gov/welcome-tucson.

7. Ernesto Portillo, Jr., "Neto's Tucson: US Policy Reawakens the Sanctuary Movement," *Arizona Daily Star*, November 15, 2014, http://tucson.com/news/local/neto-s-tucson-us-policy-reawakens-the-sanctuary-movement/article_cef2a949-89d9-58d1-9539-c888f9e1eada.html.

8. "Mission," Pima Community College, accessed May 1, 2018, https://www.pima.edu/about-pima/mission/index.html.

9. "Diversity and Inclusion," Pima County Community College District Governing Board, last modified July 19, 2017, https://www.pima.edu/about-pima/policies/board-policies/docs-bp-02/BP-2-01.pdf.

10. "Presidents Pledge," Community College Consortium for Immigrant Education, accessed August 14, 2018, https://www.cccie.org/presidents-pledge.

11. "About Refugee Resettlement," Arizona Department of Economic Security, accessed August 1, 2018, https://des.az.gov/services/aging-and-adult/refugee-resettlement/about-refugee-resettlement.

12. "Refugee Arrivals by State and Nationality," Refugee Processing Center, accessed August 1, 2018, http://www.wrapsnet.org/admissions-and-arrivals/.

13. "Refugee 101: Citywide Information Night" (presentation, Refugee Processing Center, Tucson, AZ, 2018).

14. "Refugee 101: Citywide Information Night" (presentation, Refugee Processing Center, Tucson, AZ, 2018).

15. Dick Startz, "Sealing the Border Could Block One of America's Crucial Exports: Education," Brookings Institution, January 31, 2017, https://www.brookings.edu/blog/brown-center-chalkboard/2017/01/31/sealing-the-border-could-block-one-of-americas-crucial-exports-education/?utm_campaign=Brookings+Brief&utm_source=hs_email&utm_medium=email&utm_content=41969284.

16. "Immigrant Founders of the 2017 Fortune 500," Center for American Entrepreneurship, accessed February 11, 2019, http://startupsusa.org/fortune500.

Chapter Five

Providing Equitable Education as a Daily Call to Action

Jeff Wagnitz and Rolita Flores Ezeonu

It's Monday morning, early in fall quarter. Two dozen hijab-clad women crowd the narrow entryway of a one-story structure, Building 19, at the heart of Highline College's main campus. Past the entry, across the reception area inside, a student-painted mural fills the wall on the other end of the space, some twenty feet into the building. The image portrays the faces of four women, representing different points on the globe. One is wearing a hijab.

The mural's visual message of including, embracing, and encouraging campus diversity is what we strive for in our services and programmatic offerings. Equity is our goal, and we believe that diversity is our greatest asset in getting there. Welcoming newcomers is step one.

Building 19 is home to Highline's Adult Basic Education (ABE) department, which houses English as a second language (ESL) classes, Puget Sound Welcome Back Center (PSWBC), and several transition-to-college programs. As such, it is the college's entry point for most immigrants and refugees like this group of Somali women. But Highline's commitment to its global population is campus-wide and deeply woven into the institutional culture.

In this chapter, we trace that commitment, beginning with a look back into the college's earliest years, when its values took shape. From there, we review several initiatives that represent Highline's present-day response to the region's immigrants and refugees from dozens of countries, 6,300 of whom enrolled at Highline in 2016–2017, accounting for more than one-third of our student population.[1] Finally, we identify lessons learned.

A BRIEF LOOK BACK

When Highline College opened its doors in 1961 to 385 students, it became the first community college in King County, Washington. By fall of 1964, nearly 3,200 students were enrolled either part-time or full-time, and one thousand qualified applicants had been refused admission due to limited space on the new campus, outpacing construction of new buildings.[2]

During those early years, the college's students largely represented the growing middle-class families who lived in the suburban area, tucked in the southwestern corner of the county, some twenty miles south of Seattle. White faces fill the photos in the student newspaper and yearbooks of that time. Racially and ethnically, the faculty members in those early years resembled the students. The lack of diversity was such that when a person of color did join the faculty, it made headlines in the college's student newspaper, the *Thunder Word*: "HCC Gets Black Instructor."[3]

Even in the college's early years, Highline was a welcoming place for immigrants, despite their rarity. In fact, two of Highline's most notable early alumni are immigrants, Junki Yoshida from Japan and Ezra Teshome from Ethiopia. Both attended Highline in the early 1970s and went on to become successful businesspeople, philanthropists, and humanitarians.[4] Over the years, little by little, more and more immigrants and refugees made their way to the college, fleeing wars and conflicts around the globe, economic hardship, and more. A 1980 *Thunderword* reported on 170 refugees from China, Laos, and Vietnam who had found a new life here.[5]

Then came the 1990s. In that decade, diversity on campus began its upward climb in earnest. The reasons are many.

For one, housing in the area was relatively inexpensive, making it a draw for the region's newer residents, many of them immigrants and young families. Further, the suburban area's airport-, hospitality-, and retail-dependent economy offered ready opportunity for entry-level employment. About that same time, the International Rescue Committee set up an office in Seattle and began settling refugees in Tukwila, a small city in our service area. The area welcomed Bosnians and Serbs. More Laotians and Vietnamese came, too. Next came Eritreans, Ethiopians, and Somalis. More recently, Afghans, Burmese, Iranians, and Iraqis have arrived.[6]

Today, Tukwila's residents number twenty thousand, 41 percent of whom are foreign-born.[7]

As the diversity of the area's population increased, so did the diversity of Highline's student body, rising from 25 percent students of color in 1993 to 34 percent five years later. By then, 17 percent of our students also identified as immigrants or refugees. The trend continued into the next decade. In 2003, the college had 45 percent students of color. By 2006, the number had risen to 52 percent, and in 2010, to 66 percent.[8]

Now, more than five decades after its founding, Highline is the most diverse higher education institution in the state, with more than 70 percent students of color and people representing more than 120 cultures and ethnicities. Today, Highline's 17,000 students are a microcosm of the world.[9]

FOUNDING FACULTY, FOUNDATIONAL VALUES

For many institutions, this dramatic change in demographics could be viewed as a challenge. But for Highline, a critical cultural dynamic was at work, profoundly shaping the trajectory of the institution.

Faculty who had been the backbone of the college from its earliest years had created the expectation that our college was, at its heart, a social justice institution. The initial champions were a comparatively diverse group of men who found each other on campus and clicked through their common interest. They had come from California and the central area of Seattle, where social justice issues were at the forefront.

As new faculty came on board, these early faculty leaders spread the word, sharing with others on campus their belief in justice for all, this idea of the college as a social justice institution. There were doubters and detractors, of course, but the dominant voices were strong and committed to the social justice cause. These forward-thinking faculty—who could not have anticipated the demographic and socioeconomic changes to come in the region—were critical as our institution responded.

COMMITTING VALUES TO A TANGIBLE PLAN

Although indispensable, values alone can't drive institutional change. For Highline, the transition from aspiration to tangible planning came in 1994 when, to satisfy an accreditation recommendation, the college launched a strategic planning process that included students, faculty, staff, administrators, and community members. The process sought to review the institution's strengths, weaknesses, and role in the community. The three resulting strategic initiatives revealed the college's initial effort to commit its values into a college-wide manifesto:

Initiative 1: Create a college climate that attracts, welcomes, enrolls, and retains students.

Initiative 2: Expand visibility and involvement of the college with the community.

Initiative 3: Create a college climate that values diversity and enhances global perspectives.[10]

Our mission and strategic plan guided us as Highline's diversity continued its rise. As Highline's planning became more sophisticated and data driven, its strategic goals were eventually quantified in a *Mission Fulfillment Report* that, to this day, monitors the college's success in supporting its immigrant and refugee communities. To meet those objectives, the institution has implemented a variety of interventions and has sustained a variety of commitments. The examples that follow illustrate some of these initiatives and promises.

PROGRAMMATIC RESPONSES

English as a Second Language

Nearly 80 percent of our immigrant and refugee full-time equivalent student population is enrolled in our ESL program, constituting the largest cohort of any community college in Washington. [11]

Because tuition is waived for these noncredit courses, the college forgoes more than $2 million annually in revenue. Granted, an element of pragmatism is at work here, given that without this population of students, we would sometimes be hard pressed to meet enrollment targets. But our college leadership does not use enrollment targets as a rallying cry to motivate faculty and staff to embrace the work involved in serving our ever-increasing newcomer community. Rather, the college's culture, the commitment to social justice that drives our work daily, provides the motivation. It is an intentional choice on our part.

For some students, simply improving English skills is their goal. However, we encourage them to progress to college-level courses. To meet those goals, we have piloted, refined, and institutionalized a number of programs and interventions. Some examples follow.

I-BEST

Highline College was among the first community colleges in the state to offer Integrated Basic Education and Skills Training (I-BEST). [12] The intent of I-BEST is to eliminate years of remediation work and, instead, pair basic academic skills and language courses with college-level occupational skills courses in in-demand career fields. Two or more instructors teach the courses, ensuring students are supported. Currently, Highline offers certificates in four areas: business technology, education, hospitality and tourism, and healthcare. Students choose from close to a dozen certificates, including customer service, early childhood education, hotel operations, and home care aide.

We have found I-BEST significantly accelerates student attainment of college-level credits and increases student retention. Students learning English are often frustrated by the time it takes to progress from one level to another in ESL courses. Pairing such courses with relevant content, leading to an I-BEST certificate—and employment possibilities—provides a significant motivator for student retention.

Those students in intermediate ESL, known at Highline as Level 4, can usually complete a certificate within three to twelve months. Along the way, they learn job training and college readiness, both important areas to support immigrants who are unfamiliar with college and careers in the United States. Once students complete an initial certificate, they can find employment in their chosen career, which, in turn, will help them increase their language skills on the job. Students can return to Highline to pursue additional certificates. As they add certificates—and thus credits—they gain momentum on their way to an associate degree.

Jumpstart: A Transition-Support Program for ESL Learners

Another transition-support option is Jumpstart,[13] a homegrown program started in 2010. The idea came about during a brainstorming session of our ESL-to-Credit Task Force, formed as part of our Achieving the Dream (ATD) initiative. The ATD initiative leads a national network of community colleges committed to closing achievement gaps; increasing attainment of degrees and credentials; and improving economic opportunities for their students, particularly low-income students and students of color.[14] The Highline group was trying to identify unique and innovative solutions to help our higher-level ESL students transition to college-level courses. Students apply for Jumpstart and, if accepted, receive a "scholarship," which is actually a tuition waiver.

Participants take the highest level of mainstream precollege reading and English classes, along with a supplemental support class, all tuition-free. Students who meet the outcomes of the English and reading classes are able to continue to English 101 and other college-level classes. The supplemental support class ensures that students are successful by providing a review of English and reading concepts, help with college navigation, and intensive academic advising.

There is a cost to the college, in that English and reading faculty are teaching a class that could have gone to tuition-paying students. But the program's outcomes are worth it. Data as of winter quarter 2018 show that 248 students participated in the 25 Jumpstart cohorts between winter 2010 and spring 2016. Of those students, 204 (82 percent) went on to take at least one college course; 174 (70 percent) took at least 15 credits; and 71 students (29 percent) have completed their program of study (which includes two-year degree and certificate programs).[15] There are qualitative successes, too. Faculty report students "come alive" in Jumpstart, writing more and better than they thought possible and bonding as a cohort.[16]

Off-Site Classes

Research, as well as anecdotal evidence, indicates that commute times to classes can be a significant barrier for students in deciding whether to pursue an education. That effect is magnified among basic skills learners.

According to a Washington State Board for Community and Technical Colleges study, approximately 40 percent of students in Highline College's catchment or service area travel ten minutes or less to attend college-level classes. For ESL students, by comparison, the figure is nearly 70 percent. For those traveling between ten and twenty minutes, another disparity becomes evident: close to 50 percent of students in college-level classes make that commute compared to just under 30 percent of students in ESL classes. [17]

The data show us that ESL students are more likely to travel only a short distance to attend classes, compared with all students in college-level classes. For the immigrants and refugees in our community, who juggle families, jobs, and more, even a relatively short ten- to twenty-minute commute to campus can be a deterrent. Given that immigrant communities are distributed widely across Highline's district—and that the results were similar for other metro-area colleges across the state—it is reasonable to infer that longer commute times inherently inhibit participation.

Our response has been to offer classes in strategic locations in a number of communities where students live and work. One such location is at a YWCA in White Center, a community ten miles north of our main campus. At this particular location, all students are refugees and immigrants. Approximately 150 students attend each quarter, most of whom are English-language learners. [18] At that site, our Education department offers early childhood education classes in several language cohorts, including Arabic, Somali, and Spanish. Many of the students are early childcare providers working toward their state credentials. For those students, we offer three stackable early childhood education certificates.

Our Continuing Education department also offers a variety of classes, such as home care aide, healthcare interpreter, and customer service.

Puget Sound Welcome Back Center

One of ten centers across the nation, PSWBC [19] helps internationally educated professionals recertify to work in the United States. Like many of Highline's services to local immigrant populations, PSWBC grew from the passion and good ideas of faculty and staff here.

During the 2006–2007 academic year, an English teacher in our immigrant and refugee ESL program heard again and again that her students were doctors, nurses, and pharmacists in their countries, but were working as taxi drivers, fast food workers, and warehouse employees in the United States.

She explored options of recertification for internationally educated healthcare professionals and discovered the national Welcome Back Initiative (WBI), which started in San Francisco, California, in 2001, and helps foreign-trained healthcare professionals enter related careers in the United States.

The WBI's national network consists of ten Welcome Back Centers in nine states. Five are based in community colleges, and others partner closely with community colleges or other community or adult education organizations.[20] After flying to San Francisco to learn more, the English teacher presented the idea to college administrators, who approved of starting a center at Highline. She then brought together college faculty and staff as well as community partners from a variety of organizations to make it a regional effort and help with funding.

Since PSWBC opened its doors in 2008, it has served more than 1,200 healthcare professionals, including 726 nurses. In 2014, the center began helping professionals in other fields: 230 in STEM and business fields and 140 from a variety of other occupations, including 52 teachers. All told, close to 1,600 participants have been helped at the center.[21]

Highline's approach and institutional support for the center differs from many, if not all, of the other centers. Those who seek assistance from PSWBC are called *participants*, not *students*, since those who qualify for services will often not enroll in a Highline class. They may take other courses designed to prepare for licensure exams, such as the National Council Licensure Examination (NCLEX) for nurses, but more often than not, they never become a Highline student. Instead, the center partners with outside organizations to provide services.

To help its internationally educated nurses prepare for licensure in the United States, for example, PSWBC partners with Kaplan, a test preparation company, to offer classes to prepare for NCLEX. PSWBC publicizes the course and offers free orientations during the summer. Kaplan charges $500 for the course, which includes four months of online learning and three months of face-to-face instruction from Kaplan. For those unable to pay, PSWBC looks for funding sources to offset some or all of the course and textbook costs.[22]

Having PSWBC participants enroll in classes outside of Highline's offerings was not the original intent when we envisioned the center, but it has become the prevailing practice, based on the needs of our area's immigrants and refugees. Our belief in the benefits of the center outweighs the financial downside. It speaks to our overall commitment to serving this population of our community and contributes to workforce development.

Transition Center and Working Students Success Network

In October 2008, Highline created the Transition Center to provide in-depth academic advising, financial assistance, outreach, and workshops, all designed to help our ABE/ESL students understand their educational and career options, develop plans, secure funding, and navigate the college. The Transition Center came about as the result of qualitative studies, surveys, and, again, the ideas of our employees.

Focus groups revealed that 80 percent of upper-level ESL students were interested in pursuing degrees or certificates, but knew little or nothing about what the college could offer, what it might cost, how to pay for it, or how to get started. The college's processes and programs, so familiar to the experienced local consumer, were seen as impenetrable to first-time students from faraway countries with different education systems.[23]

Offering further evidence, data from the Community College Survey of Student Engagement (CCSSE) revealed that, among immigrant students who had transitioned successfully to credit curriculum, the reliance on college support resources was high. This suggested to us that an important component of the college's strategy would be to engage these students early on with services such as advising, tutoring, and financial aid. CCSSE is administered by the Center for Community College Student Engagement to Highline students approximately every three years, providing valuable feedback to ensure institutional effectiveness.[24]

Through conversations, participants emphasized the importance of relationships with faculty, staff, and fellow students. A friendly, accessible, and knowledgeable contact person could play a significant role, students said, in helping them navigate processes and meet key people on campus.[25]

Today, the Transition Center plays an important role in the development and advancement of immigrant and refugee students by connecting these students with academic programs and leadership opportunities not only to advance themselves, but also further promote the college's mission of globalism and diversity.

The college's social justice orientation also requires that we confront income inequality, which disproportionately affects communities of color and English-language-learner communities. To integrate our response to these intersections of circumstance, the college chose to co-locate its Transition Center—as well as other support services such as Workforce Education Services (WES)—as part of the Working Student Success Network (WSSN) facility, established at Highline as part of our ATD initiative. These support services[26] are together in Building 1, located a short distance from Building 19, mentioned earlier as the entry point for most immigrants and refugees. Building 1 has recently been remodeled so that those support services are integrated with initial assessment and placement, pathway selection, and faculty advisor assignment.

Funding for support services comes from a variety of sources. Students participating in WES, for example, receive tuition and other financial assistance from the state's Employment Security Department. WSSN was initially funded as a grant, now incorporated into our base budget.

The Transition Center and WSSN actively work toward supporting the central themes to ATD, of which Highline College is currently a leader school. WSSN focuses on three areas: (1) education and employment advancement; (2) income and work supports, which include financial aid advising; and (3) financial services and asset building, such as financial education and coaching. The Transition Center directly supports the first two areas by advising students on transitioning from noncredit to credit-bearing classes, connecting students with employment and career resources, and helping students navigate financial aid options. With this synergy, students are surrounded by Highline professionals ready to support their transition, retention, and completion.

LESSONS LEARNED

Lesson 1: Build on Campus Values

The strongest arguments for institutional change develop when philosophy and pragmatism meet. We were fortunate to have that synergy during the 1990s when we undertook a comprehensive strategic planning process. Our rapidly diversifying community needed a college that could respond to its unique needs. And our college had two generations of faculty who were deeply committed to social justice. The campus was primed to accept and embrace the work. Without that synergy, any executive-level push for change would surely have fallen flat.

Over the past two decades, subsequent revisions to our mission statement and the strategic plan reflect our ongoing commitment to increase diversity and educational and social justice equity. The culture of support for our diverse community has been woven into the fabric of the college. We view providing an equitable education as a core value, a source of pride, and a daily call to action.

In fact, our college has been recognized nationally for its commitment to increasing diversity, equity, inclusion, and social justice. Highline is a four-time winner of the Higher Education Excellence in Diversity Award, the 2016 winner of the Association of Community College Trustees Equity Award for the Pacific Region, and the 2014 winner of the American Association of Community Colleges' Award of Excellence for Advancing Diversity.

Lesson 2: Create and Measure Mission-Level Commitment

The mission-level leadership environment of today that supports immigrant and refugee education owes its origins to the 1990s strategic planning process and the campus culture that nurtured it. Our strategic plan gives us a tangible tool to guide us. We then measure our progress in fulfilling the plan's initiatives using data. Those data are instrumental in finding weak spots in student attainment and prompting faculty and staff to take a hard look at curriculum and come up with new programs and interventions.

We believe in the axiom "what gets measured gets done." Anyone reading our *Mission Fulfillment Report*, and the data therein, should be able to tell what we value as a college.

Obtaining the necessary data became a priority in the 2000s.

In 2006, the MetLife Foundation named Highline as a finalist in its Community College Excellence Awards, demonstrating our campus-wide commitment to serving the traditionally underserved. At that time, based on our institution-wide work during the strategic planning process of the 1990s and a comprehensive development plan created in 1998–1999, we were able to demonstrate to the MetLife Foundation that Highline had achieved substantial gains creating successful precollege and college experiences for traditionally underserved students.

But we knew then that our accomplishments were not enough to meet the needs of ABE/ESL students, an area of steady growth. As a next step, we applied for, and were accepted into, the national AID initiative, welcoming the opportunity to further develop our culture of evidence, whereby student performance and attainment data informed our decision-making processes. Through participating in ATD, we looked to strengthen our work in four areas:[27]

- Expand and refine community-to-campus initiatives.
- Strengthen academic support services.
- Strengthen and integrate developmental education.
- Improve advising and student information services.

All four areas speak to our desire to help immigrants find success in college, with ESL transitions, specifically, a major focus.

As part of ATD's initial data-analysis protocol, we found that, as Highline's ABE/ESL enrollments grew, immigrant students were persisting into college-level coursework at a low rate. For example, the fall-to-spring transition rate (academic year 2004–2005) from ABE/ESL into college credit was less than 1 percent—a disappointing figure, but in line with national trends. Buoyed by our inclusion in ATD, we began investigating the progression shortfall of our ABE/ESL students.[28] To provide encouragement and accountability, we set a stretch goal of improving the rate to 10 percent.

Today, immigrant and refugee students' transition rates have improved. Data from 2016–2017 indicate that 4.7 percent of immigrants (N = 936) and 7.6 percent of refugees (N = 251) transitioned from noncredit to college-level courses.[29] We have work to do to meet our 10-percent goal, but the figures represent significant gains from the mid-2000s.

Data from 2016–2017 also indicate that immigrant and refugee students are completing their courses of study. In that year, these students earned 149 associate degrees, 140 certificates (ranging from short-term certificates under 20 credits to longer certificates over 45 credits), and 5 applied bachelor's degrees, which are relatively new on our campus.[30] We are confident that the increase in recent transition rates will result in an increase in completion rates in the next few years.

Lesson 3: Incorporate Pragmatism

We talked about wedding philosophy and pragmatism in Lesson 1. Here we speak more specifically about our pragmatic reasons. In addition to meeting our college's enrollment targets, mentioned earlier, three reasons come to mind, all which speak to fulfilling our mission as a comprehensive community college:

- To meet Washington state's evolving economic and workforce needs, at least 70 percent of the state's adults, ages twenty-five through forty-four, will have a postsecondary credential by 2023[31]
- To reduce the brain waste that occurs when a highly skilled individual is either unemployed or underemployed because their skills, qualifications, or education is not recognized
- To reduce the need for social services that drain resources when immigrants and refugees are unemployed and underemployed

Lesson 4: Encourage Trust and Innovation

Our collective belief in social justice paved the way to embrace the demographic changes within our student population. What was also crucially important—especially to making curricular and programmatic changes—was, and remains to this day, the college's culture of collegiality, built on strong relationships, mutual respect, and cooperation.

It is a "high-trust environment," in the words of our faculty union president.[32] It is also a high-dedication environment. On our best days, those qualities reinforce one another, fostering innovation, high expectations, and joyful hard work within a climate of mutual confidence, interdependence, and support. We want each other to succeed, not for our own sake, but for advancement of our community, our students, and our values.

In 2003, an accreditation team even made note of our culture, giving the college a commendation for our "special spirit." The team's report commended us for our collegiality, for the respect and appreciation we demonstrate to each other, and for the way we consistently demonstrate the college's values in our work and our programs.[33] Collegiality and trust nurture an entrepreneurial spirit among staff and faculty, leading to innovative programs and services designed to meet the challenges of serving our immigrant and refugees communities. The Jumpstart program is a prime example. It was developed in a safe environment for risk-taking and entrepreneurship and supported by a trusting administration.

Lesson 5: Focus on Assets

We look to fulfill the hopes and dreams of those who seek us out. Although hope is a rather nebulous concept, we find a tangible expression of it in our asset-based philosophy of working with students. We work hard to emphasize what students do know when they begin at Highline and build on those assets, rather than the deficit perspective of focusing on what they lack.

Perhaps the clearest example of this approach is through PSWBC mentioned earlier. PSWBC recognizes and works with the professional credentials and educational and work experience of newcomers. It then builds on those assets to equip newcomers for their next step toward their career, rather than having them start the educational process from the beginning.

ONE STUDENT'S SUCCESS STORY

We began our story with the Somali immigrants in Building 19, who were likely at the beginning of their educational journey at Highline. We will close with a look at one immigrant and how a few of our programs helped him achieve a significant milestone in his education.

Born and raised in Lima, Peru, Emilio originally came to Highline in 2013 to brush up on his English skills for an entry-level job. His ESL Level 3 instructor persuaded him to take an ESL transition class, enabling him to explore careers and find support for moving to college-level classes. At that point, he was still undecided. Again, with her prompting, he applied for Jumpstart and was accepted for winter 2014.

Emilio had his share of struggles, so much so that he often wondered which one was the worst. With every obstacle he overcame—learning English, developing keyboarding skills so he could complete assignments on time, and creating effective study habits, to name just three—he gained more and more confidence, creating a positive feedback loop.

He made the most out of his college experience, getting involved in our Center for Leadership and Service and the Inter-Cultural Center, where he made friends and built skills and confidence. He sought help in our Writing Center and from his instructors when he doubted his abilities. And, he took a part-time job as a reading/ESL/study skills tutor in our Tutoring Center. There, he discovered his love of teaching.

By spring of 2018, Emilio had earned an associate degree and proudly crossed the stage during our commencement ceremony, with plans to remain at Highline to pursue an applied bachelor's degree in early learning and teaching, with the goal of becoming a teacher. [34]

For immigrants like Emilio, the journey from Building 19 to the commencement stage is not without its challenges. It is incumbent upon us as an institution to continue to refine our processes and programs in an effort to improve the educational journey for these newcomers. After all, we all benefit from the assets they bring to our communities and to campus as we prepare students to live and work in a multicultural world and global economy.

NOTES

1. Emily Coates, email message to author, May 2, 2018.

2. Tim McMannon, *Our Award-Winning Campus (Buildings!): Construction in the 1960s and '70s* (Des Moines, WA: Highline College, 2012), https://www.highline.edu/about-us/highline-profiles/our-award-winning-campus/.

3. "HCC Gets Black Instructor," *Thunder Word*, February 14, 1969, https://documents.highline.edu/collections/thunderword/1969/02141969.pdf.

4. "Alumni Recognition," Highline College, accessed May 1, 2018, https://alumni.highline.edu/recognition/.

5. "Health Services Helping Refugees," *Thunderword*, May 9, 1980, https://documents.highline.edu/collections/thunderword/1980/05091980.pdf.

6. Ben Stocking, "The Revival of Foster High: School Filled with Refugees Makes a Comeback," *Seattle Times*, January 2, 2016, https://www.seattletimes.com/education-lab/the-revival-of-foster-high-a-school-filled-with-refugees-makes-a-comeback/.

7. "Quick Facts: Tukwila City, Washington, United States," US Census Bureau, accessed June 19, 2018, https://www.census.gov/quickfacts/fact/table/tukwilacitywashington,US/PST045217#viewtop.

8. *Title III Application, Comprehensive Development Plan* (Des Moines, WA: Highline Community College, 1999).

9. *Facts and Information: 2017–2018* (Des Moines, WA: Highline College, 2017).

10. *Title III Application, Comprehensive Development Plan* (Des Moines, WA: Highline Community College, 1999).

11. Emily Coates, email message to author, May 2, 2018.

12. "Washington State I-BEST and Integrative Learning Resource," Highline College, accessed August 12, 2018, https://ibest.highline.edu/.

13. "Jumpstart Program," Highline College, accessed August 12, 2018, https://precollege.highline.edu/jumpstart.php.

14. "Achieving the Dream," accessed August 12, 2018, http://www.achievingthedream.org/.

15. Bevin Taylor, email message to author, April 30, 2018.

16. Monica Lemoine, email message to author, April 12, 2018.

17. Eric Jessup and Jeremy Sage, *Washington State Community and Technical Colleges Transportation Access Study* (Pullman, WA: Washington State University School of Economic Sciences, 2009).

18. Nou Lee, email message to author, April 29, 2018.

19. "Puget Sound Welcome Back Center," Highline College, https://welcome-back.highline.edu/.

20. "Welcome Back Initiative," accessed August 12, 2018, https://www.wbcenters.org/.

21. Linda Faaren, email message to author, April 26, 2018.

22. Linda Faaren, *Feasibility Study: Welcome Back Center* (Des Moines, WA: Highline College, 2016).

23. *2009 MetLife Short Application* (Des Moines, WA: Highline College, 2009).

24. "About the Center," Center for Community College Student Engagement, accessed August 12, 2018, http://www.ccsse.org/center/.

25. *2009 MetLife Short Application* (Des Moines, WA: Highline College, 2009).

26. "Highline Support Center," Highline College, accessed August 12, 2018, https://support-center.highline.edu/.

27. *2006–2007 Achieving the Dream: Community Colleges Count Application* (Des Moines, WA: Highline College, 2006).

28. *2009 MetLife Short Application* (Des Moines, WA: Highline College, 2009).

29. Emily Coates, email message to author, May 2, 2018.

30. Emily Coates, email message to author, May 2, 2018.

31. Washington Student Achievement Council, *The Roadmap: A Plan to Increase Educational Attainment in Washington, 2013* (Olympia, WA: Washington Student Achievement Council, 2013), https://wsac.wa.gov/sites/default/files/2013RoadmapWeb.pdf.

32. Dr. James Peyton, conversation with author, December 14, 2017.

33. Dr. Priscilla J. Bell, email message to author, April 30, 2003.

34. Emilio (pseudonym), email message to author, May 1, 2018.

Reflective Narrative

No Risk, No Reward — Unlocking Opportunity in a Changing America

Suzette Brooks Masters

In 2018, the foreign-born made up nearly 14 percent of the US population, a level not seen since the turn of the twentieth century. Many of the nearly forty-four million immigrants[1] who live in the United States today arrived in the last few decades, after passage of the Hart-Celler Act in 1965. Unlike in prior immigrant waves, immigration over the last few decades has touched all parts of the country, not solely the large cities that had served as traditional immigrant gateways. Many rural and suburban areas across the country are experiencing the effects of immigration for the first time in recent memory.

Immigrants and refugees come to America for different reasons and under different circumstances, but all share a desire to thrive in their adopted homeland. However, for many newcomers the path to opportunity can be long and difficult, littered with obstacles large and small, obvious and subtle.

Community colleges are a key stepping-stone for immigrant and refugee students seeking to pursue higher education or skill building, and hold great promise to unlock their potential. Yet many colleges have been slow to respond to the changing composition of their communities and student bodies. Against the backdrop of a foreign-born population approaching historic highs and an increasingly heated and divisive debate about who is coming to America and why, many community colleges have been reluctant to wade into contentious territory, attract undue attention, and activate political backlash. So they pretended that nothing was changing at all.

Ten years ago, when I was a program officer overseeing the immigration grants portfolio at the J. M. Kaplan Fund, a family foundation in New York

City, I was looking for important levers to advance and accelerate immigrant integration. I was intrigued by the outsize role community colleges could play in fostering that integration. As I researched what programs in higher education existed for immigrants, I found precious few. One institution that did catch my eye back in 2008 was Westchester Community College in New York, which was just constructing its new Gateway Center dedicated to immigrant education after having raised significant new resources from private and government donors to make the center a reality.

I approached the leadership team at Westchester Community College with a bold idea: to launch a new organizational platform, the Community College Consortium for Immigrant Education (CCCIE) to lead the community college sector in developing, promoting, and nurturing a growing ecosystem of community colleges and systems whose programs would intentionally address the obstacles immigrants and refugees face in pursuing their education.

Little did I know then how much passion, grit, and determination would be required for all the actors committed to this work. The sector was slow to pivot, the issue continued to be polarizing, and the Dreamer movement would unleash a grueling debate about whether nearly two million undocumented young people who came to the United States as children would be able to realize their dreams of advancement in America.

The truth is that CCCIE was ahead of its time, and its Blue Ribbon Panel member colleges were at the vanguard of the country's 1,200 community colleges in proactively welcoming immigrant students—documented and not, full-time and not, fluent in English and not, heading to a four-year college and not—and designing programs specifically to help them succeed, whatever their trajectory and goals.

In many ways the struggles facing the community colleges within the CCCIE network (including Westchester Community College, which has provided consistent and generous in-kind support to CCCIE's team, and its donors like the J. M. Kaplan Fund) mirrored those of immigrants themselves. All were trying to adapt to a changing America that wasn't quite sure what to make of the rapid changes it was undergoing, to model good practices, and to empower institutions and their leaders to tackle these issues because it was the right thing to do, even if it was controversial.

We were making history, all of us—real immigrant students, real teachers, real administrators, real college presidents, real activists, and real donors. Change came slowly but, little by little, novel programs for immigrants became institutionalized and institutional resistance and fear subsided.

I am so proud that the J. M. Kaplan Fund took a risk and invested in CCCIE and maintained that support during my tenure at the Fund, that Westchester Community College took a risk and assumed the leadership of a national project that ran on fumes but had big aspirations, that the founding members of CCCIE took a risk and developed cutting-edge new ways to make their institutions work for immigrant students and to share their forward-looking practices with their peers, and that immigrants took a risk and pursued their dreams in America against formidable odds. Together, we are changing America for the better.

NOTE

1. Jie Zong, Jeanne Batalova, and Jeffrey Hallock, "Frequently Requested Statistics on Immigrants and Immigration in the United States," Migration Policy Institute, February 8, 2018, https://www.migrationpolicy.org/article/frequently-requested-statistics-immigrants-and-immigration-united-states.

Part Two

Front-Line Teams Dedicated to Success of New Americans: Designing Pathways to College and Careers

Chapter Six

LaGuardia Community College's Noncredit Pathways for New Americans

John Hunt

LaGuardia Community College's division of adult and continuing education (ACE) has played a critical role in welcoming local immigrant community members to campus and creating sustainable pathways to meet their educational, career, and family goals. As the largest continuing education division among all the City University of New York (CUNY) campuses and one of the most comprehensive in the country, LaGuardia's ACE division believes in the transformative power of education and strives to establish innovative programs that currently serve more than thirty thousand New Yorkers of diverse cultures, ages, ethnicities, and educational and economic backgrounds.

According to the 2016 American Community Survey, there were more than 305,000 adults in the New York City borough of Queens—where LaGuardia is located—who lack a high school diploma, 72 percent of whom speak a language other than English at home. Overall, 49 percent of Queens residents are foreign-born, while one-fifth of those households are limited English speaking.

Furthermore, the Migration Policy Institute reports that 94,000 immigrant individuals in Queens have foreign professional degrees but speak English "less than very well" and are consequently unemployed or "underutilized" in lower-skilled jobs (2010–2014).[1] To respond to these community needs, LaGuardia's ACE precollege programs serve more than six thousand community members annually in their high school equivalency programs (in both English and Spanish) and their English for speakers of other languages (ESOL) classes. Programs are both grant-funded and low-cost tuition.

ADDRESSING IMMIGRANTS' NEEDS

To serve low-income English-language learner (ELL) students better, La-Guardia founded the Center for Immigrant Education and Training (CIET)[2] to provide free, noncredit adult ESOL courses where lessons are contextualized to civic engagement and citizenship, immigrant parent engagement, and integrated workforce development, especially for the healthcare sector. CIET serves ELL adults drawn from a variety of its local Queens immigrant neighborhoods, such as Corona, Woodside, Elmhurst, and Jackson Heights, and as well as clients from around the city. Students enter programs at a range of English proficiency levels from total beginners to high intermediate and bring with them diverse educational backgrounds from their home countries; some do not have high school diplomas and others have professional licenses and university degrees.

Curricula for ESOL classes at CIET are contextualized to meet the communication needs of its students, with lessons focusing on such topics as reading a report card, attending parent-teacher meetings, answering questions in a doctor's office, interacting with customers or supervisors in the workplace, finding neighborhood resources on the internet, or understanding government and US history. Classes are interactive and participatory as students work on projects in pairs and small groups with the aid of qualified ESOL instructors to brainstorm ideas, explore answers together, and do research in a computer lab. Field trips and workshops led by visiting community partners allow students to connect with New York City's cultural instructions and local nonprofits to deepen their civic engagement and strengthen referral pipelines between the campus and the local community.

Goal setting and next-steps planning are integrated into the ESOL coursework to encourage students to design their own educational and career pathways, which may include high school equivalency classes, enrolling in CUNY, or entering a noncredit workforce training program. In-class workshops include an exploration of LaGuardia's own continuing education catalog to compare certification programs, tuition costs, eligibility requirements, and whether the career sectors and occupations on offer correspond to students' interests or skills sets. Faculty and educational case managers also assist students with immediate workforce goals to navigate the English required for a US-style resume and connect with local Workforce1 Career Centers,[3] which are operated by the New York City Department of Small Business Services (SBS).

To address the specific barriers facing local immigrant parents wanting to improve their English proficiency and better navigate local school systems, CIET implemented its Immigrant Family Literacy ESOL program, which provides English courses contextualized around parent engagement activities, such as reading report cards, going to parent-teacher conferences, and understanding standardized testing and the high school application process. These New York State Adult Literacy Education–funded classes take place for an average of nine hours a week, in the evenings or during school hours when parents are available, over thirty-five weeks per year.

The contextualized curriculum incorporates proven family literacy components, including adult literacy training for parents leading to economic self-sufficiency; interactive literacy activities between parents and their children; and training for parents on being full partners in the education of their children, on topics such as parents' rights and self-advocacy awareness building. To develop participants' intergenerational communication skills as well as to connect them with local community organizations, immigrant family nights are also held during which parents and their children can attend joint workshops led by cultural institutions such as the Guggenheim and Noguchi Museums.

Immigrant parents learn the language skills needed for real-life contexts, such as meetings at public schools, phone interactions with school staff members, and exchanges in healthcare facilities and libraries. Students are encouraged to bring to class samples of real-life communication (e.g., letters from the teacher, flyers, and medicine labels) so that relevant scenarios and role plays can be practiced, thus encouraging more confident communication outside of class.

As a result of these classes, parent participants have achieved above-average oral proficiency gains, as measured on the New York State Education Department's (NYSED) Report Cards for Adult Education Providers.[4] They report having attended school meetings, volunteered at their children's schools, or contacted their local parent coordinators, often for the first time or for the first time without a translator.

To bridge the digital divide that keeps many immigrant parents from accessing critical information, students also spend an average of two hours a week in computer labs with a focus on developing the skills needed to navigate online resources and participate in the workforce. Students learn to send email, use Microsoft Office, and navigate the internet in order to access NYSED websites, self-study ESOL sites, and CIET's own Connecting Immigrant Parents website, developed through a grant from the Deutsche Bank Americas Foundation to gather resources for immigrant parents in New York City.

THE NEW YORK CITY WELCOME BACK CENTER

To provide enhanced career pathways services to its noncredit immigrant students with professional skills acquired in their home countries, LaGuardia also established the New York City Welcome Back Center (NYCWBC), an affiliate of the national Welcome Back Initiative. Its mission is to assist immigrant healthcare professionals in achieving recredentialing in New York State to meet the city's demand for a culturally and linguistically diverse workforce. The center aims to help clients navigate the New York State relicensing process in their healthcare specialties; advise them about career ladders and alternative pathways in healthcare for immigrants; assess their English-language and job-readiness skills; and refer clients to appropriate English language, test preparation, professional advisement, and job placement services. The center is publicly funded by SBS, NYSED, and CUNY itself in braided funding streams, including Workforce Innovation and Opportunity Title II and Career and Technical Education Perkins funding.

The NYCWBC has played a critical role in addressing the main barriers preventing this population from advancing on their career pathways in the United States and from contributing their in-demand skills to the New York City healthcare workforce. English proficiency remains the primary obstacle for NYCWBC clients, with more than half of immigrant nurse applicants scoring below a seventh-grade English reading proficiency level during recent intake sessions, despite having been licensed professionals in their home countries. This language gap effectively prohibits these professionals from transferring their technical knowledge into English and often excludes them from US training programs where entrance exams are required.

Many become discouraged after cycling through general ESOL curriculum courses, which may not address their professional needs, and after unsuccessful attempts at passing linguistically complex US licensing examinations. Others find it challenging to navigate state-level recredentialing board requirements and transcript verification protocols. These setbacks often lead to a professional "loss of identity" crisis wherein students begin to feel trapped in lower-skilled jobs in the United States outside of their field of expertise (for an average of five years for recent NYCWBC clients).

LaGuardia has been at the forefront nationally in adapting Washington State's Integrated Basic Education and Skills Training (I-BEST) model to a noncredit workforce certification context for ELL students. The NYCWBC's "NY-BEST" courses pair ESOL teachers in a team-teaching model with technical content instructors, allowing immigrants greater access to high-growth career pathways. NY-BEST allows students at lower proficiency levels (e.g., with eighth-grade Test of Adult Basic Education[5] reading scores) to access relicensing training, which has resulted in higher student retention rates and in relicensing exam pass rates significantly above the national average for foreign-educated healthcare professionals.

In partnership with LaGuardia's Health Sciences Department, the NYCWBC's NY-BEST National Council Licensure Examination (NCLEX) Prep Course for English Language Learners trains underemployed immigrant nurses to become relicensed in New York, responding to local employer requests for healthcare workers with bilingual and bicultural skills.

LaGuardia has found that students with lower intake scores can succeed in credentialing courses, provided that adequate ESOL support is integrated into the instructional models. To best advise applicants at intake, preassessment processes also include Best Plus oral assessments,[6] writing samples, computer literacy assessments, and one-on-one panel interviews. In some cases, in-house, hard skills mini-assessments (e.g., nursing questions) are also conducted. These efforts are made to provide lower-skilled learners with the opportunity to join a training program, while avoiding the risk of admitting them into courses that might be too challenging for their proficiency levels, even with ESOL support. Although this can be considered an art rather than a science, LaGuardia's holistic approach toward assessment has been successful, and its NY-BEST courses have served immigrant nurses well.

These noncredit, grant-funded courses serve underemployed or unemployed ELL nurses in integrated and concurrent team-taught thirty-two-week cycles for an average of sixteen hours per week in the evenings. The curriculum is designed to develop the ESOL reading and communication skills required to succeed in training, on the NCLEX, and in the US healthcare workforce. It consists of intensive ESOL lessons and the development of critical-thinking skills for the healthcare sector, a thorough review of healthcare technical content by nursing faculty, NCLEX preparation, US nursing workplace and job readiness workshops, digital literacy and computer lab sessions, along with comprehensive case-management services. Lessons and in-class workshops prepare students for US classroom norms, English medical terminology, and the rigors of technical lectures, while engaging clients in intensive case-management barriers assessment and social services referrals.

Immigrant nurses completing this noncredit program have seen wage gains of more than 150 percent upon New York State licensure and average salaries of $72,000, many after being underemployed or unemployed for more than five years since arrival in the United States. Significantly, this NY-BEST model has also resulted in student persistence rates higher than 95 percent, despite intensive evening course schedules over a span of up to eight months.

The Spanish-language broadcaster Telemundo recently profiled one such NYCWBC success story. Nelly left her professional career as a nurse in Ecuador and immigrated to Queens more than a decade ago. However, she faced significant challenges in attempting to advance on her US career pathway, telling Telemundo, "The biggest barrier, as an Hispanic, was the [English] language. I felt sad and frustrated because I wanted to use my skills but I couldn't. [After failing the NCLEX exam several times], I said no, no more.

After so much effort, after the last time, with tears in my eyes, I said to my husband that I didn't want to do it anymore."[7]

But after finding out about LaGuardia's NYCWBC, Nelly was able to enroll in CIET's intermediate-level ESOL bridge courses for a year before transitioning into the NY-BEST NCLEX integrated preparation course. She successfully completed the program and finally achieved her goal of obtaining relicensure in New York and securing full-time employment as a registered nurse in a local healthcare facility.

PATHWAYS FOR CONTINUING EDUCATION

Another key component of LaGuardia's continuing education services for its local immigrant populations are ACE's adult basic skills and high school equivalency bridge to college and careers departments, which aim to provide educational pathways for students who were unable to attain their secondary education diplomas in their home countries. These departments prepare students for New York State's challenging high school equivalence (HSE) exam, the Test Assessing Secondary Completion (TASC).

Formerly administered through the general equivalency diploma, TASC is offered in both English and Spanish on campus through LaGuardia's state-funded HSE Testing Center. LaGuardia's HSE and adult basic education courses contextualize lessons around workforce sectors and college majors, such as healthcare and business, while also offering comprehensive college and career advisement services.

However, to ensure that these students view a high school diploma as just a first step in their educational pathways, transition to college support is built into the program design, with services offered in a highly engaging and practical manner. Enrollment milestones, such as completing financial aid applications, taking CUNY placement exams, and submitting immunization records have previously been barriers to students' matriculation. By working collaboratively with campus admissions, testing, and health offices, continuing education staff have established interlocking support to students as they transition from HSE to credit pathway courses.

Instructional and advisement staff have integrated college application workshops into HSE classrooms at much earlier stages than in prior years, while targeted messaging (via e-blasts, texting, and timely in-person advisement) have become more frequent and uniform across programs. Staff has also increased best-bet program advisement (i.e., those providing strong academic support services to high-need students, including those with remedial course needs) to students prior to TASC testing.

For the last three years, LaGuardia has partnered with CUNY's office of academic affairs to host "Mapping Your Future" events for its HSE students.

These panel forums include HSE program alumni who have successfully transitioned into credit courses sharing their experiences, challenges, and recommendations, while cross-divisional departments outline their services for students who may be in need of developmental education remediation, academic language immersion, admissions advisement, and job readiness.

These efforts, along with enhanced communication strategies among campus stakeholders, have increased college-going rates within LaGuardia's HSE programs. The number of divisional HSE students and alumni completing the CUNY application for enrollment in credit programs grew by 95 percent over a recent two-year span, while actual matriculation in credit-pathway programs increased by 105 percent.

LESSONS LEARNED

Although each of the programs described here has its individual complexities, some commonalities and lessons learned have emerged. For example, to establish and sustain its noncredit immigrant-serving programs, LaGuardia's continuing education division has relied on both internal and external partnerships with key stakeholders, including campus departments, local community-based organizations, national immigrant networks, and its state and municipal agencies. The technical and subject-matter expertise required to create effective contextualized ESOL curricula and workshops has come from such diverse sources as campus credit faculty, Free Application for Federal Student Aid advisors, parents rights organizations, and national immigrant professional networks.

Outreach and enrollment for potential applicants are made possible through dissemination of program flyers via these same networks and through local adult education coalitions, borough-based immigration tasks forces, local workforce development boards, and, above all, through the positive word-of-mouth of successful former students in their local immigrant communities. As with many grant-funded, noncredit programs, securing sustainable funding has represented a significant challenge, so active communication and reporting with state and local government agencies on both the need and influence of programs has been a consistent priority.

To facilitate those discussions, the development of data collection and tracking protocols represents a core component of the success of both launching and sustaining programs. LaGuardia began this process organically through informal conversations among staff, instructors, students, and wait-listed applicants, along with basic case management services for its general ESOL and HSE populations.

As common demographics and barriers emerged—such as difficulties navigating parent-teacher conferences, reflecting foreign professional experience on a US résumé, or transitioning into credit programs—departments began implementing more targeted intake and wait-list application forms, preassessments, student surveys, and case-management tools. In this way, LaGuardia was able to demonstrate to potential funders that a need existed for programs serving such groups as immigrant parents, foreign-trained healthcare workers, and HSE Spanish students seeking transition to credit. The data also provided a baseline for confirming the subsequent effects and outcomes of these services.

Another factor that has emerged in the success of LaGuardia's continuing education immigrant-serving programs has been the role of its embedded educational case managers. When combined with high-quality, contextualized instruction and effective intake procedures, case management has proven itself critical to maintaining student persistence and success, especially for programs with significant numbers of instructional hours where participant attrition and transition to next-steps goals achievement have been challenging in the past.

These services often begin at intake when case managers lead information and enrollment sessions and then evolve into both workshop sessions with ESOL and HSE classes, as well as one-on-one consultation sessions during the semester. Workshops focus on short-term and long-term goal setting, stress management, and techniques for developing self-advocacy skills, especially for navigating challenging bureaucracies or immigrant rights. Individual sessions cover more in-depth needs assessments and barriers analysis with clients and may involve referrals to campus departments or local partner agencies for crisis intervention on such topics as mental health or domestic violence.

LaGuardia Community College recognizes its role in creating educational and career pathways to meet the needs of both its credit and noncredit immigrant students. By leveraging the resources of its campus departments, community and government partners, and immigrant-focused networks, its ACE division has succeeded in providing effective services for its local ELL and high school equivalency immigrant students at multiple levels of proficiency, from those who were professionals in their home countries to those who have not yet been able to achieve a secondary school diploma.

NOTES

1. Margie McHugh and Madeleine Morawski, *Immigrants and WIOA Services: Comparison of Sociodemographic Characteristics of Native- and Foreign-Born Adults in Queens County, New York* (Washington, DC: Migration Policy Institute, April 2016), 5, https://www.migrationpolicy.org/research/immigrants-and-wioa-services-comparison-sociodemographic-characteristics-native-and-foreign.

2. "Center for Immigrant Education and Training," LaGuardia Community College, accessed August 22, 2018, https://www.laguardia.edu/ciet.

3. "Workforce1," New York City Department of Small Business Services, accessed August 17, 2018, http://home2.nyc.gov/html/sbs/wf1/html/about/about.shtml.

4. "Accountability Reporting," New York State Education Reporting, accessed August 17, 2018, http://www.acces.nysed.gov/aepp/accountability-reporting.

5. "Tests of Adult Basic Education," accessed August 17, 2018, http:/tabetest.com. TABE is used by educators to assess the skills and knowledge of adult learners.

6. "Best Plus 2.0: Assessing Adult English Language Proficiency," accessed August 20, 2018, http://www.cal.org/aea/bp.

7. Liz González, "Inmigrantes, Talentos Desperdiciados (primera parte)," *Telemundo47 Responde*, WNJU, February 14, 2018, https://www.telemundo47.com/responde/Inmigrantes_-talentos-desperdiciados-primera-parte_TLMD---Nueva-York-474177853.html.

Chapter Seven

Accelerated Pathways for Immigrants in the Rio Grande Valley

Juan Carlos Aguirre and Matthew Hebbard

South Texas College (STC) is uniquely situated in an international context along the southern border with Mexico, the Rio Grande Valley. The context of the region is not defined by political boundaries, as there are shared historical, cultural, linguistic, social, and economic influences on both sides of the border. The region serves as a gateway between North America and Latin America where the immigrant experience is understood and supported.

For decades, immigrants have come to this region in search of a better quality of life for themselves and their families. STC serves this population with innovative and accelerated programs. This chapter describes two of these programs: (1) an Integrated Career Pathways (ICP) program that has greatly expanded educational and employment opportunities in high-demand fields for the region's low-skilled adults and English as a second language (ESL) learners who lack a high school diploma, and (2) a comprehensive dual-credit program that has significantly increased graduation rates of the many high-skilled undocumented students residing in the Rio Grande Valley.

DEMOGRAPHIC BACKGROUND

ST serves more than 31,000 credit students and 24,000 noncredit students each year in a two-county service district in the Rio Grande Valley region of South Texas. In terms of demographics, 95 percent of the college-credit student population is Hispanic and most students receive some form of financial aid. Many students are the first in their families to go to college. The Rio Grande Valley region is a bicultural and binational region given the close proximity to Mexico. Many students are first-, second-, or third-generation as they may have immigrated to the United States themselves or have parents, grandparents, and great-grandparents who were immigrants.

The college does not track Deferred Action for Childhood Arrivals (DACA) recipients but usually serves between eight hundred and nine hundred undocumented students, according to state reporting measures. Undocumented students and recent immigrants are served through the college's dual-credit programs; however, the exact number cannot be confirmed prior to high school graduation and matriculation into higher education. The Supreme Court decision in *Plyer v. Doe* allows students the right to a public education regardless of immigration status. As a result, student immigration status is not tracked by local high schools and is not determined until students apply for college using the statewide admissions application referred to as *ApplyTexas*. Students who may be undocumented are able to participate in dual credit programs and attend college in Texas while paying in-state tuition. Students may identify themselves as undocumented through the college application process.

Many students are bilingual and are enrolled in heritage Spanish courses, which are Spanish-language courses for native speakers of Spanish rather than second-language learners. The majority of ESL learners are served through the college's noncredit continuing education programs. For intermediate-level ESL immigrant students who have low literacy skills in their native languages, the college offers noncredit programs that integrate ESL and general equivalency diploma (GED) or high school–level instruction with contextualized industry credentials and marketable skills. The programs increase retention rates by accelerating time to completion and the increasing opportunity for meaningful employment. In addition, students are able to continue into credit programs through the conversion of noncredit hours to credit programs as the contextualized instruction they have received is aligned with credit courses and taught by credit faculty.

For high-skilled undocumented students, including Dreamers and DACA recipients, the college offers a comprehensive dual-credit program for more than fourteen thousand students. The college waives tuition and fees for these students and provides the opportunity for them to earn up to sixty hours or more toward an associate degree at no cost. The dual-credit program includes early college high schools, dual-enrollment academies, and traditional dual-credit classes offered at comprehensive high schools. Early college high school students take a combination of courses at the high school and the college campus to earn an associate degree or sixty credit hours toward a bachelor's degree at the same time they graduate from high school.

Dual-enrollment academies, which are focused on specific professional fields, begin in the junior and senior year and are year-round so that students stay in a cohort with their peers and graduate with associate degrees as seniors in high school. Traditional dual-credit students normally focus on core academic classes such as English, math, and government or career and technical education classes and take classes at the high school during their junior or senior year. Dual-credit students have full access to college courses and college support services at the high schools and on the college's campuses. Thousands of undocumented students participate in dual-credit programs each year and are more likely to matriculate into higher education and graduate with degrees because of the opportunity and support they receive from dual-credit programs.

INTEGRATED CAREER PATHWAYS

Throughout its history, the ICP program at STC has been supported by a variety of funding sources. The program started in 2009 thanks to a grant from Jobs for the Future, a national nonprofit, and its Breaking Through initiative, which has strengthened the efforts of community colleges that assist low-income, low-skilled adult learners seeking occupational and technical postsecondary credentials.[1] Between 2011 and 2016, the Texas Higher Education Coordinating Board, through its Accelerate Texas initiative, funded STC's ICP program. The objective of Accelerate Texas was to allow low-skill, low-literacy adults to co-enroll in programs that helped them earn secondary and postsecondary credentials simultaneously.

In 2013 the Lower Rio Workforce Development Board awarded STC a grant to expand career pathways in the region through Project GROW (Growing Regional Opportunities for the Workforce), which was funded by the US Department of Labor. Between 2015 and 2017, the Texas Workforce Commission, through its Adult Education and Literacy program, awarded STC several grants that allowed the college to further expand career pathways via three initiatives: (1) Accelerate Texas; (2) Texas Adult Completion and Skills Initiative, designed to enroll students concurrently in either high school recovery or high school equivalency programs and an occupational skills award (OSA) program consisting of one to three credit courses bundled into a credential; and (3) Ability to Benefit, a provision of the Higher Education Act that allows individuals without a high school diploma or equivalent to qualify for federal financial aid for postsecondary education when they participate in an eligible career pathway.[2]

STC's ICP program was designed to allow underprepared students (low-skill, low-literacy) without a high school diploma or GED to enroll in credit-bearing postsecondary occupational programs while acquiring basic literacy skills. Two tracks have been developed to assist this group of students.

Track 1 serves students functioning at the eighth-grade level in reading, writing, and math, and at the exit level in ESL, which is the most advanced noncredit ESL level. Students are co-enrolled in contextualized GED instruction and the credit-bearing OSA program, while integrating college success and employability skills, such as note-taking, test-taking, and study skills, as well as résumé writing, interviewing skills, and work ethics. Student outcomes include GED attainment, college credit hours, enrollment in a college certificate program, and employment.

Track 2 consists of two phases. Phase 1 serves students functioning at the sixth-grade level in reading, writing, and math, and at the intermediate-ESL level through contextualized ESL, pre-GED, and bilingual occupational terminology instruction. Students exit this phase functioning at the eighth-grade level in reading, writing, and math, and at the advanced exit-level ESL. Phase 2 co-enrolls students in contextualized GED instruction and the credit-bearing OSA program (i.e., Track 1), while integrating college success and employability skills. Student outcomes include GED attainment, college credit hours, enrollment in a college certificate program, and employment.

Knowing that the GED alone opens the doors to both financial aid and entry-level employment, STC has also developed a third, shorter-term track for those students who do not have the time to participate in lengthier ICP training. These students are functioning at the eighth-grade level in reading, writing, and math, and at the exit level in ESL. This track enrolls students in contextualized GED while integrating college success and employability skills. Student outcomes include GED attainment, enrollment in a short-term college certificate, and employment. While Track 1 takes approximately four months, Track 2 normally ranges from six to eight months depending on the OSA program selected, and Track 3 typically takes two months.

Of all the cohorts that have received training through STC's ICP program, one stands out in terms of tenacity and achievement: the pharmacy technician program, which is offered regularly each year and usually includes a cohort of eleven to twelve students. During the fall 2013 semester, fifteen students lacking secondary credentials and functioning at the intermediate level in ESL enrolled in the pharmacy technician program. All fifteen completed the program, which consisted of advanced ESL, GED, and pharmacy technician trainee preparation; fourteen earned their GED, ten earned college hours and became pharmacy technician trainees, and ten entered employment. Like the rest of the program's students, these fifteen had dropped out of high school years ago, had families to support, and were underemployed, but had the desire to break the cycle, better themselves, and set a new standard for their families. Furthermore, students who complete this program are now equipped to continue along a pathway with stackable credentials leading toward additional career opportunities and increased wages.

The OSA program is the first component of the career pathway and is offered through continuing education. The OSA program is essentially a subset of the certificate program and consists of one- to three-credit courses packaged into a marketable skills credential contextualized to a specific career pathway and leading to employment. Because the OSA is taught by credit faculty and consists of credit courses, the continuing education units (CEU) earned by students are converted to semester credit hours (SCH) once students attain their GED and enroll in a college certificate program.

The following career pathways, illustrating the transition from noncredit CEU courses to credit SCH and a college certificate, have been developed and are offered to this group of students:

- Certified nurse assistant to patient care assistant certificate
- Phlebotomy to patient care assistant certificate
- Medical receptionist to medical office specialist certificate
- First responder to emergency medical technology (EMT) basic certificate
- Health information management clerk to electronic health record specialist certificate
- Pharmacy technician trainee to pharmacy technology certificate
- Electrician's helper OSA to electrician assistant certificate
- Heating, ventilation, and air conditioning (HVAC) and refrigeration technician's assistant OSA to HVAC and refrigeration technology certificate
- Pipe welding to combination welding certificate
- Accounting assistant to accounting clerk certificate

These programs eventually lead to an associate of applied science (AAS) degree at STC.

A FIRST RESPONDER TO EMT AAS PATHWAY

One successful strand is STC's EMT pathway. There is high demand in the field, and it offers excellent potential for career advancement and a living wage. STC revamped its program in 2011 to allow multiple exit and entry points to accommodate the real-life events and changing needs of students. One such change was to create a new entry-level "first responder" course. As Figure 7.1 illustrates, this course allows lower-skill students to start targeted technical skills training in a credit-bearing class. The course includes college and career success skills instruction, as well as employability skills. This course leads directly to employment in a high-demand occupation, feeds into the next level credit-bearing certificate, is recognized by employers as a marketable skill credential, and can be converted to SCH. At that point, students can take a certification exam and apply for financial aid, while continuing to accumulate stackable certificates toward the ultimate goal of EMT AAS degree.

At the next level in the track—EMT basic certificate—a college prep academy component is added concurrently, preparing students for academic

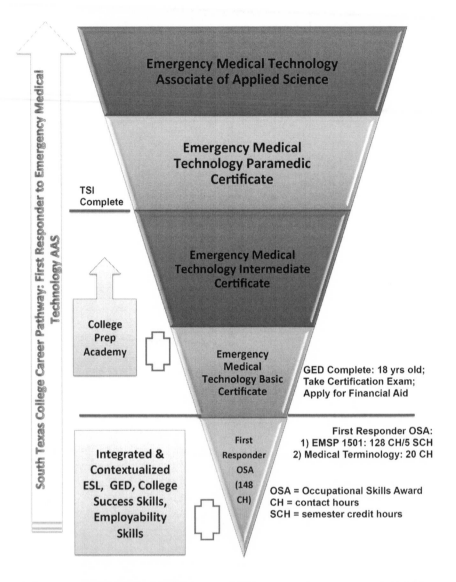

Figure 7.1.   South Texas College Career Pathway: First Responder to EMT AAS. Reprinted with permission of South Texas College.

success at the college level. The college prep academy consists of instruction in reading, writing, and mathematics designed to prepare students to take and pass the college entrance exam known as the *Texas Success Initiative Assessment*. Upon passing this exam, students are considered Texas Success Initiative–complete and are able to pursue higher certificates such as the EMT paramedic or the EMT AAS degree.

Key Success Factors

Without this highly integrated program that helps students accelerate their time to completion, these low-skill, low-literacy students would have had to take the traditional linear route: first ESL, then adult basic education, followed by the GED, and finally a college certificate program. The ICP program at STC is the only one of its kind in Hidalgo and Starr counties. What makes this program effective, successful, and special is attributed to these program hallmarks:

Working closely with Academic Affairs deans and program chairs to design continuing education certificates that feed into credit-bearing certificates and to establish the process for converting CEUs to SCH, thereby allowing students to move through the career pathway without having to repeat any courses.

Working with Academic Affairs program advisory committees to validate and approve new continuing education certificates that feed into credit-bearing certificates, thereby creating stackable credentials, which create a sequence of credentials that can be accumulated over time to enable individuals to move along an educational pathway or up a career ladder.

Collaborating with Centers for Learning Excellence to provide tutoring and student success workshops to continuing education students.

Collaborating with Student Affairs to provide services to continuing education students in the areas of advising, counseling, financial aid, registration, career exploration, and job placement.

Working with Student Affairs to organize employer advisory committees to review career pathways, deliver instruction, provide clinical and practicum sites, motivate students, and interview students for job opportunities.

Collaborating with Workforce Solutions (the local workforce development board), school districts, community-based organizations, faith-based organizations, and other community agencies to provide comprehensive supportive services to participants, such as childcare, transportation, materials, and supplies.

Providing intensive and intrusive case management that includes the following:

- Monitor daily class attendance: locate those absent, ascertain reasons for absence, determine corrective actions (childcare, transportation, etc.), and identify preventive measures.

- Monitor daily academic progress: identify those failing or at risk of failing, ascertain reasons thereof, determine corrective actions (tutoring, supplemental instruction, etc.), and identify preventive measures.
- Monitor daily life issues: identify those with imminent problems, ascertain causes, determine corrective actions, and identify preventive measures.

Program Outcomes

Approximately three hundred students have participated in ICP training at STC since 2011. Documented performance is as follows:

- 98 percent program completion
- 75 percent earned college hours
- 70 percent attained their GED
- 77 percent enrolled in a college certificate program or entered employment

The average cost per student participating in ICP training is $3,500. To date, the vast majority of the costs have been incurred by grants from Jobs for the Future, Texas Higher Education Coordinating Board, Lower Rio Workforce Development Board, and Texas Workforce Commission. Students have had to pay only a minimal amount, primarily in testing fees.

Knowing that grant funds are finite and are meant only to assist colleges to start up and implement new initiatives, STC has developed a sustainability plan using the Texas Public Educational Grant to continue serving low-skill, low-literacy students in the ICP program after the grants ended. The college is proud to have launched its first sustainable career pathways track in May 2014. Twelve students were selected for a phlebotomy/GED program. STC used Texas Public Educational Grant funds to pay for both phlebotomy and GED training, and students paid for their tests. Upon successful completion, students attained their GED, received two credit hours toward the medical assistant technology certificate, passed the national phlebotomy certification exam, and enrolled in the certificate program. Since then, the college has served more than one hundred students through its sustainable model.

So many lives have been touched by this program. The college's motivation to continue serving these students comes from their heartfelt testimonials. Often students say, "I never thought I would come to school," or "I thought it was too late." Quite frankly, if STC does not help these students, it is unlikely they will find assistance elsewhere. The program has become a beacon of hope for the marginalized and the forgotten. When certified nursing assistant student Lupita stated, "I didn't think there was an opportunity for somebody without a GED to get back into college," it became clear that this program epitomized that opportunity for so many folks living in the region. STC is committed to continue helping low-skill, low-literacy students earn postsecondary certificates and degrees of value in the regional labor market.

As STC continues its own journey and as other colleges embark on similar initiatives, it is necessary to point out that the biggest challenges the college faced serving this population were to find funding to assist them and to find institutional resources to sustain the program after external funding ran out. As a result, one of the lessons learned was to establish a sustainability plan early on to continue serving this population. Other lessons learned that have helped improve and enhance the program include the need for a strong daily case management system to help participants successfully navigate college, work, and life in general; and the need for a robust support system within the college built on commitments from all divisions and departments.

DUAL CREDIT FOR DREAMERS

In 2001, Texas was the first state to pass a Development Relief, and Education for Alien Minors (DREAM) Act for undocumented students in higher education. The move allowed colleges and universities to admit Dreamers and charge in-state tuition rates provided that they met the requirements of Texas high school graduation or a Texas GED and the thirty-six-month residency requirement prior to high school completion. Around the same time, the college began to grow and rapidly expand dual-credit offerings. The college now serves more than fourteen thousand dual-credit students in seventy-eight high schools including early college high schools, dual-enrollment academies, and traditional dual-credit offered on high school campuses. Thousands of students have graduated with a degree or certificate credential from the dual-credit program while earning a high school diploma. The college waives tuition and fees for students, which has saved families millions of dollars.

Even with the opportunity of in-state tuition and access to state grants, Dreamers still struggle with the costs of a college degree, living expenses, and economic needs for their family members. According to a recent study, 9 percent of the total undocumented population in Texas lives in the Rio Grande Valley, exceeded only by the Dallas–Fort Worth metroplex and the Houston metropolitan area.[3] In Hidalgo County, one of STC's two service counties, only 6 percent of the undocumented population have earned a college degree and only 9 percent have earned some college hours,[4] yet double that amount—18 percent of the undocumented population—are high school graduates.[5]

Addressing Financial Barriers and Emotional Stress

The most significant barriers to college completion for Dreamers are the financial and economic factors. In addition, these students are under psychological and emotional stress because of their uncertain status in the country and the continual political battles regarding a solution for their predicament.[6] College teams work within the local high schools and communities to help Dreamers and their families apply for college and complete the Texas Application for State Financial Aid. These initial steps can be overwhelming to students who live with uncertainty and fear.

STC staff provide sessions on financial literacy so that students develop a strong plan for success. The college also participates in various scholarship programs for Dreamers including TheDream.US and the Instituto de Mexicanos en el Exterior Becas program in partnership with the local Mexican consulate in McAllen. These generous scholarship programs provide students with financial assistance to pay for college and other expenses. The college developed a dedicated scholarship office that provides one-on-one counseling sessions to help students complete scholarship applications and stay on track to earn their degree.

As a result, the college recruitment and financial aid teams work closely with high school counselors and administrators to make students feel welcomed. Staff are from the community, are bilingual, and are sensitive to the needs of Dreamers and their families. Additionally, given the context of the region, many students who are citizens or US residents may be from mixed-status families where a parent or a sibling may be undocumented while the student is not. This community-based outreach approach allows students and families to connect with the college early on and get to know a staff member who can help them with the process.

Students and families are welcomed on campus and are made to feel a part of the college community. Faculty are often a part of the outreach effort and are active in supporting the needs of the students. In a more recent initiative, the college has partnered with local advocacy groups to help undocumented students know their rights as students and provide resources to support them in their educational journey. Such events have provided safe spaces for undocumented students and families to ask questions and to be more informed about resources that can help them. Under the student affairs department, the college offers the services of licensed professional counselors who are trained staff members equipped to help Dreamers and DACA recipients who are under emotional or psychological stress due to their immigration status and the uncertainty of federal policies that directly affect their personal lives and academic performance.

Providing Accelerated Degree Pathways and Fast-Track Events

Through the dual-credit program, the college provides accelerated and affordable pathways to degree completion. Dreamers are able to participate in all three major programs offered by the college: early college high schools, dual-enrollment academies (many focused on STEM fields), and traditional dual credit focus on core academic courses. Dual-credit students may also participate in a variety of career and technical education courses such as robotics, computer applications, and skilled trades. The college awarded almost 1,200 associate degrees in the 2017–2018 academic year to dual-credit students, who earn a college degree before high school graduation.

One of the most important distinctions of the dual-credit program is the comprehensive student services provided for all dual-credit students. Student services staff members are assigned to work with local high schools by geographic regions and have developed key relationships with school principals, teachers, and counselors. In 2017, as a part of the Dual-Credit Enrollment Services department, student services staff coordinated with school district personnel to pilot online registration for dual-credit students. Staff organized specific days, by high school, for new dual-credit students to attend a fast-track event on the college campus. School districts provided the transportation and coordination during the regular school day, and counselors partnered with college staff to organize applications, student portal credentials, orientation, and online registration.

The enrollment services team at the college had completed a major redesign of the business processes, services, physical space, and technology in collaboration with institution informational technology teams and facilities staff. The redesign provided an open-space, friendly environment in which to serve students in an enrollment center concept. Dual-credit fast-track events were organized around the enrollment centers to provide the opportunity for dual-credit students to become familiar with college services and processes while still in high school. The events also included campus tours and overviews of on-campus services and degree programs. After the pilot semester, fast-track events were rolled out to all districts including all dual-credit students and graduating dual-credit seniors transitioning to the college. The initiative is intentionally designed to promote student engagement and student connection to the college early on, so students know what services are available to them when they transition from high school and are encouraged to matriculate to the college after high school completion.

Dreamers and DACA students represent one of the most at-risk populations in terms of matriculation. Through the fast-track events, the college provides access and equity for these students as they are treated equally along with the other dual-credit students and are able to find helpful and friendly staff at the college and become familiar with college-going processes. At the same time, outreach and admissions frontline staff have been trained to address the special situations and challenges faced by immigrant students, especially Dreamers and DACA recipients. Students are guided through the processes of using the online student portal, accessing their early-alert profile, reviewing their degree audit, and registering for courses all online. The college staff and counselors work closely to create an inclusive environment and reassure immigrant students that, regardless of their status, they can go to college and will be supported.

Dual-Enrollment Academies

One particularly notable dual-credit model is the dual-enrollment academies[7] program. The academies are two-year dual-enrollment programs for high school juniors who are interested in earning an associate degree at STC during their junior and senior years of high school. The college offers five dual-enrollment academies in medical science, engineering, criminal justice, computer science, and business administration. The academies are a cohort model and students must complete a separate application as the programs are competitive and limited in capacity. Students must meet certain requirements to be able to apply, as well as submit letters of recommendation from their high school teachers and counselors. The college sets high expectations for student achievement and at the same time provides personalized services, such as academic advisement, mentoring, and coaching to all students in these programs.

The academies staff also organize college visitation trips outside of the area to institutions such as University of Texas–Austin, Texas A&M, and Baylor University to inspire at-risk and undocumented students and help them gain the confidence they need to transfer to selective and Tier 1 universities. The cohort model, staff assistance, and proactive interventions support undocumented students and build their confidence to succeed.

Dual credit has served as a key strategy to ensure that more undocumented and immigrant students go to college and even have the opportunity to earn a college degree while in high school. These efforts not only help students who are at risk of dropping out of high school because of the pressures that immigrant students face, but they also increase the college-going rate for this population of students. Students are connected to college courses and services early on in their high school career, and when they graduate from high school, they continue on to complete their degrees at the college or they transfer to a university to complete a bachelor's degree at a substantial cost savings.

HELPING IMMIGRANT STUDENTS AND FAMILIES REACH THEIR POTENTIAL

Twenty-five years ago, STC began as a community-led and state-supported institution to affect the lives of the people of the Rio Grande Valley and improve the quality of life for all. Inherent in this vision is the immigrant community, which has been vital to the growth and economic vitality of the region. Through the college's credit and noncredit programs, many immigrant students and their families have earned certificates, degrees, and other credentials that have provided living-wage jobs and meaningful careers. The ICP program helps low-skilled immigrants and ESL learners develop language and career skills to give them a pathway to employment and career advancement in high-demand occupations. The dual-credit program has provided tuition-free college courses for high school students who earn college credit for transfer and associate degrees prior to high school graduation. Both programs provide clear and seamless pathways for immigrants in the community at all educational levels in order that they may have a better quality of life and be able to support their families. Faculty and staff are always on hand to support students and to help them believe in themselves to reach their full potential.

NOTES

1. "Breaking Through," Jobs for the Future, accessed August 13, 2018, https://www.jff.org/what-we-do/impact-stories/breaking-through. The Breaking Through initiative was launched in 2005 by Jobs for the Future and the National Council for Workforce Education with funding from the Charles Stewart Mott Foundation.

2. "New Guidance on 'Ability to Benefit,'" Office of Career, Technical, and Adult Education, US Department of Education, https://sites.ed.gov/octae/2015/06/05/new-guidance-on-ability-to-benefit.

3. Alexa Ura and Jolie McCullough, "Interactive: Demographics of Texas' Undocumented Population," *The Texas Tribune*, January 28, 2015, https://www.texastribune.org/2015/01/28/undocumented-population-demographics/.

4. Ura and McCullough, "Interactive."

5. Ura and McCullough, "Interactive."

6. Kaitlin Mulhere, "Undocumented and Stressed," *Inside Higher Ed*, January 26, 2015, https://www.insidehighered.com/news/2015/01/26/study-finds-undocumented-colleges-students-face-unique-challenges.

7. "Dual Enrollment Academies," South Texas College, accessed August 13, 2018, https://academicaffairs.southtexascollege.edu/highschool/academies/index.html.

Chapter Eight

Helping Skilled Immigrants and Refugees Transition to Jobs

How Pima Community College Taps Unrealized Workforce Talent

Adam Hostetter, Montserrat Caballero, Norma Sandoval-Shinn, and Regina Suitt

Some immigrants and refugees arrive in the United States with degrees in hand and years of professional experience, looking to translate their foreign education and experience into a viable career path in the United States. Often, these skilled individuals end up unemployed or working in low-wage, low-skill, survival jobs. This significant "brain waste" in the skilled immigrant population is occurring while many open jobs are going unfilled because there aren't enough qualified candidates to fill them.

Educational institutions like community colleges should be the place for new immigrants and refugees with degrees from their home countries to look for guidance. After all, an academic institution should be a natural resource; it's a place immigrants and refugees with degrees can recognize! Yet community colleges are a uniquely American phenomenon. And for many immigrant and refugee students, the community college is not a natural first place to go for help.

Many times these degreed professionals or business experts lack only English or knowledge of American workplace culture and vocabulary to be able to get jobs and thrive in their new communities. Pima Community College (PCC) in Tucson, Arizona, addresses these needs through its Transition to US Workforce program. Begun in 2013 in partnership with JobPath, a local workforce nonprofit, Transition to US Workforce provides support for immigrant and refugee residents of Pima County, including Tucson, who need assistance transitioning to college-level education and job-training programs that lead to a living wage.

In 2016, PCC inherited this successful program from JobPath and has embedded it as a noncredit class offering. Run by the Transitions to US Workforce team—which includes dedicated, experienced volunteers; the volunteer coordinator; and an immigrant college and career navigator—PCC's Transition to US Workforce program offers a low-cost and replicable approach to assisting foreign-educated immigrant students to navigate college services and prepare for skilled jobs.

IMMIGRANT DEMOGRAPHICS AND PROGRAM DESCRIPTION

The Tucson metropolitan area, where PCC is located, has nearly one million people; more than 13 percent of the population is foreign-born.[1] Arizona is the fifth-highest resettlement state for refugees as well. A significant percentage (35 percent) of Arizona's foreign-born population ages twenty-five and older have less than a high school credential, and many are not literate in their native languages. However, a sizable amount (20 percent) have some college or an associate degree, and 22 percent hold a bachelor's degree or higher.[2] Mexico is Tucson's largest source of immigrants. Tucson and Mexico share culture and families, regardless of where the borders have moved. Less than half of Tucson's foreign-born residents are US citizens.

Transition to US Workforce fits into a larger picture at PCC within the Adult Basic Education for College and Career division. The division serves more than six thousand students per year, meaning it serves one-fifth of the total student population at the college. The Adult Basic Education division is critical in serving both the native-born population without educational credentials and the thousands of foreign-born individuals who have limited English skills. The bulk of the programming includes adult basic education, adult secondary education, and English-language acquisition for adults.

On top of that foundation, the division also offers a "rights and responsibilities of citizenship" course for students who want to naturalize, as well as a large refugee education program for refugees resettling in Tucson. In fiscal year 2017, the refugee program served nearly eight hundred students resettled from twenty-seven countries. In 2018, the program served five hundred with concentrated numbers from Congo, Syria, and other African countries. This stark decrease is due to new eligibility requirements and changes in the number of refugees being admitted to the United States.

A SUSTAINABLE MODEL WITH STRONG OUTCOMES

Participants come to Transitions to US Workforce from countries all over the world, including Bangladesh, Chile, China, Colombia, Congo, Cuba, Eritrea, Iran, Iraq, Israel, Japan, Mexico, Peru, Puerto Rico, Russia, Spain, Syria, Togo, and Ukraine. For each immigrant or refugee who finds employment that aligns with his or her skills and experience rather than an entry-level job, the increase in salary represents thousands more in economic contribution in the community and strengthens the labor market. Immigrant success in the American workforce also opens more opportunities to their children.

From 2013 to 2018, nearly half of the Transition to US Workforce graduates moved into jobs in accounting, business, chemistry, dentistry, education, human resources, international trade, microbiology, and wastewater engineering. Others are in postsecondary occupational programs, Test of English as a Foreign Language, preparation programs, volunteering, or they have continued taking English-language classes.

Alicia was a participant in the Transition to US Workforce program from July 2013 through September 2014. She came to the United States from Mexico with a degree and previous work experience in microbiology. "Because of this class, I improved my skills," Alicia said. "Now I have more confidence to communicate in the regular day-to-day activities and at a professional level. I have learned about cultural protocols and community activities that have helped to update my knowledge. I have had all the support of volunteer coaches at all the steps of my job-seeking [process]."

After improving her English, Alicia worked as a University of Arizona community health worker with a Hispanic women's research project, then at PCC as a science lab specialist. After completing the Transition to US Workforce program, she entered training to become an environmental and health specialist at the Pima County Health Department, where she is currently employed as a communicable disease investigator.

One of the most exciting aspects of PCC's model is sustainability. Small student cohorts matched with three volunteer facilitators not only keep budget costs low, but also provide for teacher-to-student ratios that allow for personalized support. Small student cohorts also allow for flexibility in scheduling. Utilizing available open spaces in existing facilities outside of normal class times makes good use of classrooms.

The volunteer coordinator is a paid, full-time position in the program. Once the program was running, the coordinator was able to dedicate a small number of hours weekly to maintenance and support. The other paid position is an immigrant college and career navigator. Investment in the navigator was essential for success, but utilizing the expertise of an existing full-time English as a second language (ESL) instructor allowed the Transition to US Workforce team to have insights from an ESL professional, as well as someone who continues to work in the classroom. The navigator is paid for ten hours per week to support the cohort and maintain connections with the local one-stop system, job market information agencies, and employers.

SYSTEMS NAVIGATION—EXPECTATIONS VERSUS REALITY

Transition to US Workforce is offered as a free noncredit class for highly skilled adult immigrants and refugees who are able to speak, read, and write English at an intermediate level or higher. They must have a certificate or college degree from another country and be legally authorized to work in the United States. Most participants are already students at PCC, studying English in the English-language acquisition for adults program, which is part of the college's Adult Basic Education division. Participants are recruited internally from the division's English classes.

Transition to US Workforce classes are held at the PCC location that has the largest population of English-language learners and is home to the Refugee Education Program, convenient to a large number of immigrants and refugees with critical employment requirements. The location also houses significant ESL programming and is centrally located in Tucson and accessible by public transportation.

The immigrant college and career navigator supports systems navigation, acting as a resource on aspects of job readiness and college knowledge that are unique to or more complex for immigrants. Support in systems navigations is a critical piece of the Transition to US Workforce success story.

On a practical level, systems navigation in Transition to US Workforce starts with a reality check: an in-depth and individualized check-in on the expectations students have regarding career prospects in the United States. Many come to the program assuming that a little improvement in their English is all they need. Most understand that they will need a résumé, have to apply for jobs, and attend job interviews. Some have the awareness that getting their documents evaluated and learning where the job openings are is important. However, hardly anyone is aware—or ready—for the intense labor required to get a professional job in the United States.

Learning the Knack of "Selling Themselves"

Finding a job requires a combination of knowledge of US work culture and, importantly, the language ability to project themselves successfully as worthy candidates. For example, students find the concept of "selling themselves" difficult to understand. It may feel like bragging, which is not an appropriate part of many of their cultures. In addition, the challenge of becoming proficient at selling yourself is a skill difficult to master. That's why, in Transition to US Workforce, volunteer facilitators help students overcome these challenges by providing multiple opportunities for practice and ongoing feedback for improvement in both group and individualized coaching sessions.

Many students have great difficulty in promoting their past employment experiences. A good example is David. His quiet demeanor and inability to adjust to the American characteristic of "self-promotion" deflected the volunteer facilitators' attempts to identify his relatable strengths in regard to developing a resume. It was several weeks into the class before it was actually understood that he had been the supervisor for a United Nations refugee camp of more than 180,000 people. He was in charge of food distribution and health promotion classes. Because of the skills he developed doing this work in the refugee camp, the United Nations sponsored him to come to the United States.

The volunteer facilitators had to dig this information from him. It took many weeks to incorporate David's vast skill set into his "elevator speech," résumé, and mock interview answers. He had been working as a cook and janitor in a local restaurant up to that point. Certainly, in part, because of the facilitators' success in identifying this past work skill set, he was subsequently hired into a professional position by a Tucson nonprofit organization.

Facing Outside Pressures and Trauma

It took facilitators a while to recognize that their students are adults and have other pressures—such as families, jobs, and lack of transportation—to integrate into their class requirements. One of the adjustments facilitators made was to hand out a complete course handbook that included the content for each class session along with relevant articles. This handbook allows students to read up on the material for any missed class, which subsequently keeps them from falling behind in course content.

Aside from these normal pressures, there can be more serious circumstances that affect students' lives. One example is Diomo's remarkable story. Diomo came to the United States from the Republic of Congo, where he had a stable family and professional life that literally ended overnight.

In 2016, during the first open election in many years, Diomo supported the successful candidate for president. However, the ruling dictator, Sassou Nguesso, canceled the results of the election and started hunting for anyone whom he deemed the "opposition." Diomo had to flee, and his family had to hide in the jungle to escape government troops. Diomo applied for and received asylum in the United States. He had to face the pressures of a new culture and the Transition to US Workforce class, all the while not knowing what had happened to his family.

The family was able to get out of the Republic of Congo and into a large refugee camp in a neighboring country, where it will take almost a year to process them into the United States. His family is still at risk, and if identified, they will be sent back to their home and jailed or possibly murdered.

Under these circumstances, Diomo worked diligently, attending class every week, and meeting with every teacher outside of class to review his résumé, practice interviewing, and search for jobs. He requested an additional tutor, with whom he also met twice a week, to practice advanced English conversation. He got a library card and checked out books on US culture and job searching and researched all he could on the internet. Thanks to his determination, Diomo applied for and was offered a job as a chemical engineer in New Mexico, where he relocated in late 2017. He is awaiting the arrival of his family in late 2018, provided all goes well.

Other challenges for students include the concept of tailoring a résumé to fit different positions or to address the values of the potential employer. When practicing in a mock job interview, students struggle to illustrate how their qualifications match the requirements described on the job posting. They often ask, "Why do I need to say that? That information is on my résumé!" The curriculum teaches students specific language and workplace skills, and shows them how to access community and online resources. Teachers continually check in with students to make sure that they understand how things are different and how to adapt to the expectations of this culture.

Understanding the Varying Purposes of Credential Evaluation

An important part of being ready for college and careers in the United States involves translating and evaluating foreign college credentials, which is neither cheap nor easily accessible to all students. Recent arrivals to the United States might not yet have access to a credit card, which is the most common form of payment taken by companies that provide these services, which are often available only online. Transition to US Workforce helps students understand that there are different types of evaluations with varying costs.

Examination of the types of evaluation, their varying purposes, and considering individualized needs is a student-by-student process on which the small class cohort and volunteer or navigator can spend quality time. Whether it is proving equivalence of a degree, a course-by-course evaluation necessary to apply to graduate school, or applying with a specific employer, being clear on the purpose of the evaluation is crucial so students do not end up wasting financial resources.

Additionally, students need to be aware that, even when dealing with accredited evaluation companies, not all evaluations will be accepted everywhere. For example, one of Tucson's local school districts only accepts evaluations done by their own preapproved companies. Facilitators and the immigrant college and career navigator steer immigrants with backgrounds in K–12 education to work from that list of evaluators. This requires an in-depth awareness of the local labor market and employers, which is part of the role that volunteer facilitators and the navigator bring to the class. Individualized attention to the specific situation of each student allows for a more useful reality check. Before students embark on the cost and effort of translation and evaluation services, they must understand whether such use of resources is advisable.

Each student's situation is unique, and individual processes need to be tailored to the student's needs and aspirations. The reality check helps the student understand his or her path and provides a structure for program staff to dig deeply into the reality of who this student is and what he or she needs.

CREATING CURRICULUM

The Transition to US Workforce class has flourished thanks to the three dedicated volunteer facilitators who worked together to develop and revise curriculum designed to assist with career development in the United States. The individual volunteers brought many years of training, skills, and experience in high school and university teaching, in addition to career development experience.

The target audience for the curriculum is immigrants and refugees with degrees, certificates, or training from their home countries. Starting with a welcome and overview of the class, an introduction to cultural differences in career searches in the United States is a critical part of day one. One of the most challenging aspects of these differences for immigrant professionals, regardless of their level of education, is self-promotion and marketing, along with other cultural challenges that are different from what is considered appropriate in their home cultures.

Transition to US Workforce follows the Adult Basic Education division's four ten-week sessions (one per academic quarter). Classes meet on Fridays to avoid any conflict with the division's English classes that meet Monday through Thursday. Most Transition to US Workforce participants are also continuing their English language studies throughout the week. The curriculum has to be specific to address language and culture barriers that this unique group of immigrants faces.

The volunteer facilitators developed the curriculum in collaboration with the immigrant college and career navigator, who is also an ESL instructor in the program, and PCC's volunteer coordinator. Resources inherited from the originator of the program, JobPath, provided a jumping-off point.

Each class period focuses on a different topic. Every class session starts with "elevator speeches," followed by the career topic of the week, and each concludes with small-group interaction—two to four students work individually with a volunteer facilitator. The facilitators also identify online resources related to the classroom topic of the day. Students are expected to read the resources online before class and come prepared to ask questions or discuss what they read. A packet called the Student Guide is provided to each participant. The guide outlines the course and has all of the reading that students will be expected to do. It includes handouts on the topics covered in class including résumés, networking, and job interviews.

"Elevator Speeches" Help with Career Goals and Speaking Skills

All students in Transition to US Workforce express the goal of improving their English-speaking skills as one of their priorities. The Student Guide and each class include opportunities to speak, listen, read, and write in a relaxed environment. Public speaking confidence and abilities are a critical piece of being ready to participate in the US job market.

This is why the process of having participants develop elevator speeches begins immediately. Students use their elevator speeches in every class session to introduce themselves and practice. A thirty- to sixty-second introduction, elevator speeches are a brief and succinct self-promotion activity that teaches students to explore and communicate carefully which skills and strengths they bring to employers.

Practicing weekly, students are required to memorize their speech and work inside and outside of class until it flows naturally. With the support of the volunteer facilitators, the speech serves to improve pronunciation, enunciation, and general speaking skills. Students are made aware that a common interview question is, "Tell us about yourself," and that the time and effort they put into their elevator speech will give them a ready-made answer. The elevator speech is also a practical jumping-off point for students to start developing their résumés.

In almost every case, the new students are shy about their English skills. During their first few elevator speeches, they speak quietly and haltingly. With encouragement and practice, by the third or fourth class they are projecting their speeches with more confidence. They come to understand that they normally need to slow down and speak distinctly. Carroll, a volunteer facilitator with a background in drama, does a wonderful presentation regarding how to form words and how to project with confidence.

Facilitators explain that they are not trying to be rude, but that they need to point out pronunciation deficiencies. It is worth noting that in nearly every instance, the students are most concerned about their pronunciation and convey a strong desire to learn how to express themselves so that they can be understood. It is always noteworthy and gratifying to observe how each student's confidence improves as the class progresses.

Practicing Job Search and Interviewing Skills

Job search strategies start in the third class and include networking, job fairs, online job boards, and internships. Job search engines, such as www .indeed.com, are demonstrated for students so they become comfortable using web-based searches to explore the job market.

Part of that exploration includes an activity where each student finds a job that they may be interested in applying for. Careful reading and conversation regarding that job and the specific job posting builds vocabulary and awareness of the links between the student's current skills and background and what the employer is seeking. The next step turns to writing practice: participants build a résumé unique for that job description. Facilitators work with students to demonstrate how to use phrases from the job announcement and how to shape and word their own qualifications and experience in a way that directly addresses the qualifications being sought.

Participants are explicitly taught social media skills. Facilitators encourage students to create LinkedIn profiles and join job-seeker interest groups within LinkedIn. By week four, the résumé focus ends with an opportunity for public speaking. Students unveil their résumés to the class through formal presentations.

More subtle and complicated communication skills are also introduced and demonstrated, for example, "working a room," making appropriate eye contact, and developing conversation skills. Through group and one-on-one interactions, students have opportunities to work with native speakers to experience what these situations are like, to overcome some apprehension and develop cultural awareness around the expectations for what is appropriate to share and how to use cocktail party–type environments, interviews, and other human encounters to put their best foot forward.

Cover letters and thank you notes are covered toward the end of the course, along with discussions about using the internet and how job-seeking has changed because of the internet. The last two weeks introduce interview skills and specific practice with job interviews. The intent is for every student to practice doing a job interview at least twice. Reflection takes place on how to dress, and students are expected to make an attempt to come dressed and prepared as if for a formal interview. By the end of the course, facilitators see a major boost in participants' self-confidence.

"Interviewing for a job can be a huge source of stress and anxiety, and for me, a nonnative English speaker, this stress can be even higher," notes Diomo, a past program participant. "The Transition to US Workforce program was so helpful for me. We worked on the most common interviewing questions and practiced how to answer them. I also learned some basic information on how to get started creating my own answers. Moreover, we reviewed my cover letter. Now I possess strong interviewing skills that will make me stand out from the crowd. So I strongly believe that I will make a stellar impression at any job interview."

Flexible Class Schedules

Care is given to ensuring conflicts with ESL classes are avoided. The class typically has a sixty-minute structured time, where the weekly topic is introduced and covered, followed by sixty minutes of small-group work. The course outline is adjustable since the length of each session can vary. The facilitators have been able to conduct the class in as little as six weeks, or for the entire ten weeks of a regular session. Since students are adults, they have lives outside of class and may have other responsibilities, including running a household and working in jobs with varying weekly schedules. The lives of adult students can affect attendance and the facilitators work with this reality.

The availability of the Student Guide helps students keep up with assignments. The curriculum and the schedule are ever changing with the needs of individual students and the instructional goals of the volunteer facilitators. The facilitators may also schedule time to meet one-on-one or in small groups with students at times outside of the regular class schedule for additional support, introduction to resources (such as public libraries), and even field trips to the Pima County One-Stop Career Center or local employers.

"When I joined the Transition to US Workforce class I didn't know how to do an interview or build a résumé because everything was new to me," reported Olivia, a Transition to US Workforce student from Cuba. "These classes were a great opportunity to learn all about the process of getting a job in the USA. Now I'm working in a job that allows me to improve my English-language skills, and I'm taking English classes before applying for a position that is in line with my degree."

GAINING US WORK EXPERIENCE THROUGH VOLUNTEERING

Volunteering is a common activity in the United States. According to the Corporation for National and Community Service, roughly one-quarter of the US population volunteers in some fashion.[3] In many countries around the world, however, the concept of volunteering is not a part of either the personal or professional life.

For highly skilled immigrants transitioning to a job in the United States, volunteering is a great first step to becoming familiar with the US workplace. In the Transition to US Workforce class, volunteering is presented as a viable option for program participants. Many of the students in the class have decades' worth of hard and soft skills that would be valuable to an employer, but that experience is challenging to translate since it is all from their countries of origin. Volunteering is presented as a way to get their foot in the door and develop US-based experience. Having a volunteer job puts a US-based position on students' résumés, and allows them to develop references, another concept that is often unknown to many students, as they are not used in many countries around the world.

Benefits of Applying for and Gaining US Volunteer Experience

Often, organizations and institutions that use volunteers vet potential candidates similarly to prospective employees. Applications, interviews, and even background checks are common practice. The experience of going through these steps is invaluable to highly skilled immigrants as a low-stakes way to practice all they learn in the Transition to US Workforce class.

Volunteering allows students to gain US experience, practice their English, explore career opportunities, and improve their résumé. It allows students to learn about the community they have moved to and interact firsthand with many different native English speakers, exposing them to local idioms and phrases. It also teaches intangible things about workplace culture in the United States that are hard to convey through classroom presentations, such as expected interactions with co-workers; how to interact with clients, customers, and the public; how to address a supervisor and the higher management or administration; how to fill out paperwork; and what the typical flow of a workday might be like.

The PCC program's volunteer coordinator is proud of her role as a reference for employment seekers. She was able to highly recommended Margarita when Margarita applied for a job within Pima County's largest school district. Margarita, from Mexico, was a participant in the first Transition to US Workforce cohort. As a result she gained the confidence to apply for a position through AmeriCorps as a teacher's assistant and tutor. She completed a year of service, and then stayed on as a volunteer classroom aide. That experience on her résumé was a big reason why she was an attractive candidate for a teacher's aide. In February 2018, Margarita was hired at an elementary school. Her direct classroom experience; leadership experience; and practical skills learned such as teamwork, public speaking, and meeting facilitation helped her to get this job.

Volunteers are often a first pool of potential employees for many organizations. They have been vetted and have been trained. Students who volunteer consistently with an organization could be hired if a position opens. This is a tantalizing prospect for the Transition to US Workforce students who are eager to be employed.

Creating Profiles on Volunteering Sites and Connecting with PCC Adult Basic Education

Students who are interested in volunteering are encouraged to create profiles on volunteering sites such as VolunteerMatch (volunteermatch.org), and to apply for positions based on their skill set or careers they may be interested in pursuing. The Transition to US Workforce class also connects students to volunteering within PCC, a benefit of having the college's volunteer coordinator assist with the class.

In 2018, two past participants applied to be volunteers and are assisting their fellow students with computer and tutoring help. Maria from Chile is a computer lab assistant gaining valuable skills both in instruction and technology. Guadalupe from Mexico started as a volunteer computer lab assistant and is now running an advanced-level conversation group for English-language students at one of PCC's large learning centers located within the Adult Basic Education division.

BENEFITS FAR OUTWEIGH PROGRAMMING CHALLENGES

Transition to US Workforce is not without programmatic challenges. Although small class cohorts are beneficial for volunteer facilitators and students, recruitment and marketing is a constant need. The vast majority of English-language learners who enroll in PCC's English-language acquisition program come with low language skills and without certification or degrees from their home countries and therefore do not meet the requirements of the Transition to US Workforce program. And economic forces often pull students from the basic ESL program once they have achieved their survival-skill English goals, such as reading schedules, writing checks, or telling time.

Finding the right volunteer facilitator is critical for making the program work. Volunteers need to be flexible, teachable, and willing to work as a team. The team at PCC brings years of genuine skills in education, business, and career development. Careful screening is key, but getting the right chemistry is an art rather than a science.

Diverse funding is also a key aspect, as well as a challenge. Transition to US Workforce is supported partly through county-designated funds, Workforce Investment and Opportunity Act funds pay for PCC's immigrant college and career navigator position, and the college covers the volunteer coordinator's time. The retired volunteer facilitators continue to offer a critical connection to student success. PCC plans to develop deeper relationships with community college advising and career centers, public libraries, and the county One-Stop Career Center to assist with job searches, career counseling, and training for student job seekers.

The exciting aspects of Transition to US Workforce far outweigh the challenges. The program is replicable, sustainable, and has a strong influence on students' lives. It supports individuals arriving in the United States with degrees and years of professional experience, helping to translate that education and experience into achievable career paths. Tapping the unrealized workforce potential addresses a community concern among employers that well-paid jobs are available but qualified candidates are hard to find. Families and the community benefit, not least by helping people move from unemployment or low-wage, low-skill survival jobs into family-sustaining careers.

NOTES

1. "Immigrants and the Economy in Tucson Metro Area," New American Economy, accessed September 4, 2018, https://www.newamericaneconomy.org/city/tucson.

2. "Arizona-State Immigration Data Profiles," Migration Policy Institute, accessed August 17, 2018, https://www.migrationpolicy.org/data/state-profiles/state/language/AZ#.

3. "New Report: Service Unites Americans; Volunteers Give Service Worth $184 Billion," Corporation for National and Community Service, accessed August 17, 2018, https://www.nationalservice.gov/newsroom/press-releases/2016/new-report-service-unites-americans-volunteers-give-service-worth-184.

Chapter Nine

The Montgomery College Experience with Workforce Education for Adult English-Language Learners

Donna Kinerney

"Every time I would go to a job interview, they said I needed more experience. I finished the [MI-BEST] program; now I have a good job . . . and I am proud."—Abdel, certified apartment maintenance technician graduate [1]

Montgomery College in Montgomery County, Maryland, serves a diverse community with a wide range of learning and life needs. Experiences like those of Abdel, who moved to the United States from the Ivory Coast in 2010, are powerful reminders of the role the college can play in helping community members move forward. Indeed, underpinned by a shared value of radical inclusion, the first line of the college's mission statement, "We empower our students to change their lives," has never been so important. [2]

One way to live out this mission is through workforce readiness and career pathways programming; these are on the rise as the college seeks to meet both a broader swath of community needs and a more specific set of labor market demands. This chapter describes the evolution of a subset of this programming—the workforce English for speakers of other languages (ESOL) programs—and discusses how it serves Abdel and others, with a focus on the insights and lessons learned over time.

DEMOGRAPHICS

Montgomery County, Maryland, is a suburb of Washington, DC, and is home to a large and diverse immigrant community. From 2010 to 2014, 39 percent (309,000) of the county's total population of 794,000 residents older than age sixteen were foreign-born. Thirty-seven percent of the county's immigrant residents were from Latin America; 36 percent from Asia; 16 percent from Africa; and 10 percent from Europe.[3] Of all the foreign-born residents older than age sixteen, about 125,000 (40 percent) have limited English proficiency (LEP). Educational attainment in this group ranges widely. Of the LEP population ages twenty-five and older (117,000), a target population for adult workforce training, 32 percent have less than a high school diploma; 25 percent have a high school diploma or equivalent; 16 percent have some college or an associate degree; and 27 percent have a bachelor's, graduate, or professional degree.[4]

Serving community members since 1946, Montgomery College enrolled nearly 33,000 individual students in credit programs in fiscal year 2017 and 24,000 in workforce development classes.[5] The college offers three types of English-language programs—life and civic skills, workforce readiness, and academic English—to address a wide range of learner goals. Together these programs served more than nine thousand unduplicated students in fiscal year 2017.[6]

HISTORY OF WORKFORCE ESOL PROGRAMS

Workforce readiness and career pathways programming has recently become of great interest to Montgomery County, a region that traditionally has focused on college readiness for youth. Adults, however, have long been served by the college's Workforce Development and Continuing Education (WDCE) division. The largest programs supporting immigrants and refugees in particular are two federally funded adult education grants; both were originally administered by the local school system but shifted to Montgomery College in 2005–2006, a move that afforded grant program staff the opportunity to collaborate with other college units to expand services and attract new workforce-related funding that resulted in additional programming. Today, these programs are all under the Adult ESOL and Basic Skills for College and Careers (AEBSCC) unit in the WDCE division at Montgomery College.

The Montgomery County Refugee Training Program, funded by the US Office of Refugee Resettlement and the Maryland Office for Refugees and Asylees, has had a long history of innovation dating to the 1980s and is a solid foundation for today's workforce ESOL programming. In the early days of the program, refugee adults studied in English-language classes contextualized with customer service training. As part of their coursework, students ran their own full-service snack bar, taking orders, preparing hot drinks and snacks, and selling these small items to their peers at break time. Interested program graduates could continue to hands-on vocational and English coursework in electronics assembly, also offered by the Refugee Training Program, and then on to local employment as assembly technicians.

As employment in electronics assembly disappeared, the Refugee Training Program in 1995 developed a certified geriatric nursing assistant program that was enormously popular and provided a laboratory for refugee program staff to learn about best practices for workforce training delivery. Students were accepted into the program after an English assessment and interview to determine their oral English proficiency, understanding of the job, and their interest in working with senior citizens. As a cohort, they enrolled in a bridge class that covered vocabulary and study skills to prepare for the course, then took the content course with tutoring or a companion English class, completed their clinical hours, and finally took a test-taking practice class before certification and eventual employment.

The Refugee Training Program, still in existence, features robust relationships with area refugee resettlement agencies that provide a range of services to address family self-sufficiency needs. Agencies provide employment services that are responsible for assisting refugees with job development and placement. Partnering with these agencies has greatly informed the Refugee Training Program's understanding of employment needs for English-language learners and best practices for employment services work.

During the same period, Montgomery County's adult ESOL program, serving the community since 1952, focused more broadly on English for life skills. After moving from the school system's administration to Montgomery College in 2005 and being informed by the experiences of the Refugee Training Program, the Adult ESOL and Literacy Grant (AELG) program began offering a series of workforce-contextualized English classes, utilizing Workforce Investment Act funding and a US Department of Education contract. An ESOL for customer service class, offered with support from what was then the Montgomery County One-Stop Center, culminated in a National Retail Federation certificate. Courses in ESOL for building trades jobs, ESOL for healthcare jobs, and a later bridge to technology jobs serve as on-ramps into related classes that offer labor market–recognized credentials.

In 2010, Montgomery College and four other Maryland community colleges began working with the Annie E. Casey Foundation to expand the range of workforce training models offered in Maryland.[7] Piggybacking on Washington State's successful experience with the Integrated Basic Education and Skills Training model, Maryland developed its own model relevant to the Maryland context.[8] The Maryland Integrated Basic Education and Skills Training (MI-BEST) model features joint instruction at the noncredit level with a focus on high-demand occupational areas using content area and adult ESOL/basic skills instructors; integrated curricula; employment, academic, and support services; and embedded labor market–recognized credentials. Each college adapted these components over time to align with their particular local priorities and parameters.

As part of this work, the AEBSCC unit at Montgomery College received funding from the Annie E. Casey Foundation to pilot a nursing assistant class using the MI-BEST model. Later the Community Foundation of the National Capital Region awarded the college a grant to implement the model for a certified apartment maintenance technician program in collaboration with the National Apartment Association Education Institute and the college's Gudelsky Institute for Technology Education. During the same period, with the ongoing support of the Annie E. Casey Foundation, the Maryland community colleges joined together with their local workforce investment boards and programs in Georgia, Texas, and Connecticut to receive a 2012 US Department of Labor (DOL) Workforce Innovation Fund grant, "Accelerating Connections to Employment," to test the model empirically.[9]

Montgomery College's nursing assistant program saw a 93 percent completion rate with treatment group members earning an additional $5,518 annually over the control group one year after the program.[10] As grant funding for these projects came to a close, the Montgomery County Council, now a key backer for this kind of programming, provided continued support that allowed the college to maintain services for two cohorts per year in nursing assistantship and two in apartment maintenance, to track outcomes data, and to expand on new partnerships.

This ongoing work contributed to a US DOL H1-B TechHire grant in 2016. This new grant, targeting immigrants wishing to enter the information technology field, features three tracks, including a CompTIA A+ course, which prepares individuals for entry-level computer technician positions. The course is taught with a coteaching model and a variety of boot camps, along with English-language support, employability skills, career navigation, and job development services. As a result of this work, the AEBSCC unit now has a place at the table in the college's information technology training ecosystem.

These years came with their successes and their challenges, to be sure. Most recently the AEBSCC unit staff has been working to understand and address new requirements under the federal legislation that funds the AELG program. Replacing the Workforce Investment Act of 1998, Title II of the federal Workforce Innovation and Opportunity Act of 2014 (WIOA), with its Integrated English Literacy and Civics Education program, requires an "integrated education and training" component,[11] a "service approach that provides adult education and literacy activities concurrently and contextually with workforce preparation and workforce training."[12]

The AEBSCC unit, like so many of its counterparts in colleges across the United States, is in the process of determining the fit of existing programming to new regulations and using these experiences to revision programs and courses, so that they align with funder expectations. With those factors in mind, the following lessons learned are offered as food for thought as programs move forward.

ARTICULATING PROGRAM VALUES AND PRIORITIES

Over these years of programming, staff members have encountered a number of questions and assumptions from a range of stakeholders about who is served, how they are served, and what is taught. From the AEBSCC unit perspective, it has become clear that the unit values underpin much of the work and decisions and that articulating them internally and sharing them widely can address questions like these before they become issues, while simultaneously helping to create understanding and buy-in for the work at hand.

As educators, AEBSCC staff members value maintaining a learner-centered focus that addresses student needs and interests with a grounded understanding of what students will need to be successful in the American workplace. The practical application of this value of grounded learner centeredness becomes apparent, for example, when choosing training sectors. Staff prioritizes training in fields that will likely result in higher-paid employment for students or with better benefits (e.g., scheduling, health insurance, a career pathway) than students' current opportunities. Priority within this category goes to training in which students have expressed an interest or might have an interest with appropriate career information and guidance. Finally, as a matter of practicality in a time of limited funding, staff members seek to address sector needs rather than those of an individual employer.

Establishing and defending these priorities is, of course, a balancing act with no perfect solutions. When nursing assistant work was viewed by a funder as a dead-end job, program staff members were able to present a compelling argument for continuing programming based on this value of grounded learner centeredness, explaining that there is continued and enormous student interest in nursing assistant work; high-quality, short-term training with jobs immediately at course completion; scheduling that allows for people to work and address family responsibilities; jobs with tuition reimbursement; and work that introduces students to healthcare careers.

In making the case, the staff provided a consistent, reasoned response based on values and supported by evidence, a response that resolved funder concerns. In the meantime, with the understanding that the nursing assistant students will need further opportunities, staff members continue to seek out additional training for these students and advocate at the college and within in the community for career pathways.

MAKING PARTNERSHIPS WORK

To address student needs, the AEBSCC unit has collaborated over time with a number of external organizations, including community-based groups, re-settlement agencies, employer associations, individual employers, and government agencies, such as the local workforce entity. Internal college partners have included other academic and WDCE units. The most straight-forward partnerships typically result in cross-agency referrals—the AEBSCC unit program refers students to services outside of the college such as mental health support, and partnering agencies refer potential students to the unit for training. In more intricate partnerships, the AEBSCC unit has joined with other agencies with mutual service needs to share funding, address common outcomes, or both.

Understanding and Communicating Goals, Mission, and Values

Regardless of the type of the relationship, it is well worth the time to discuss mission and values from the outset to ensure that there is a real match be-tween agencies. For a meaningful partnership to evolve, each participating partner needs to feel that the project clearly aligns with its needs and goals on some level. Deeply engaged partners will then go out of their way to make the project work as they have some stake in its success.

On the one hand, it is important to acknowledge how the project supports each partner's mission and values. Agency values can differ widely, of course, from one partner organization to another. For example, in the AEBSCC unit's experience, federally funded agencies in the refugee resettle-ment system, driven in part by a need to address employment outcomes, have long endorsed a "work first" philosophy, creating a tension point with Eng-lish-language educators who traditionally felt that competence in English was needed prior to employment. Understanding this as a potential area of conflict allows staff to address it proactively during the planning process.

Employers, even at the sector level, will also have sets of missions and values to be acknowledged. For example, AEBSCC unit staff members have long observed that a core value for those in the healthcare sector (e.g., em-ployers, nursing faculty) is to provide superior quality and compassionate healthcare. Thus, a key strategy to establishing relationships with healthcare partners, both academic and employer, is to articulate from the outset how the project will identify compassionate participants and emphasize high-quality training with a focus on care-provider ethics. On the other hand, it has been equally important to articulate the AEBSCC unit's parameters early and clearly in the discussions.

Indeed, the early days of "partnerships" felt lopsided with more agency requests to receive services than offers to support unit programs and students with high-quality services. Now articulating the college's value for student success, staff members seek out partners with a proven record of achievement, ideally serving immigrants and refugees. Staff members advocate boldly for students, for high-quality services, and for meaningful contributions to projects. In one case, this meant walking away from a partnership with a major employer when they would not meet a targeted wage outcome for a proposed project.

Establishing Shared Accountability

Finally, the unit has observed that partnerships are most effective when there are clearly articulated lines of responsibility and shared accountability. At its best, each partner clearly understands the project's mission, its role in the mission, the expected outcomes, the timelines, and the consequences of falling behind. Whether in an oral agreement or spelled out in an memorandum of understanding or a contract, the a number of elements are best discussed in advance.

Over the years, staff members have encountered challenges with the branding and marketing of programs by partners; coordinated employment engagement and unintended competition between partners for jobs; data sharing and privacy concerns (e.g., Family Educational Rights and Privacy Act [FERPA]); agency legal obligations (e.g., Title IX) that differ; student and teacher conduct issues; partner staff conduct issues; referral processes; and targeted students to be served, particularly with respect to language level and previous educational background in the country of origin. These scenarios are all now discussed at the outset, so that everyone is clear on which agency's policies will be enforced under which circumstances; these decisions are included in written agreements when appropriate.

INVESTING IN ROBUST OUTREACH AND INTAKE

Since the early days of the Refugee Training Program's initial experiences with the nursing assistant program, it has been clear that new arrivals needed in-depth support with career and educational information and service navigation. Often students came with little understanding of the healthcare sector, hearing only from their friends that there were good jobs and that they could go to a private nursing school and become a licensed practical nurse.

Many immigrants and refugees still arrive with little understanding of the education or workforce systems in the United States; indeed, in some countries, people are so severely limited in their opportunities that the plethora of choices in the United States can be overwhelming and difficult to navigate. In other cases, friends and families in the United States influence people to choose certain jobs, regardless of how that career matches with the person's interests and needs. Thus, the need for information is enormous in order for immigrant and refugee students to make informed decisions for their futures.

These needs can be addressed through a comprehensive and robust student outreach and intake system, now a key component of the workforce ESOL programming at Montgomery College and a common goal for the original Maryland community colleges developing the MI-BEST model. This system aims to identify students who are committed to a particular sector and direct them to a service level that best matches their career interests, level of readiness, and scheduling availability, all with the goal of completion and employment success.

In the AEBSCC unit, outreach and intake, particularly at the MI-BEST level of coursework, is a multistep process that generally occurs over two or three meetings, where participants return over time to dig deeper into career information, educational pathways, and program expectations. This multistep process is intentional; to make an informed decision about enrolling in an educational program, especially one that is career-directed, most people need time to consider what they have learned, the opportunity to discuss the options with their family and friends, and time to plan for childcare, transportation, and work schedules.

Consequently, the workforce ESOL community orientation sessions often focus on sector areas rather than specific classes. They are designed to offer initial basic information to everyone regarding the career area and program or course eligibility. A participant might return for the next step or might not; not returning is not viewed as a problem, as it means the participant got the information needed to make a decision. Orientations are never a waste of time; down the road, that same participant might refer a family member or friend who is a match.

Once a person applies, depending on the funder requirements, they are asked for a number of documents to establish eligibility. Applicants then typically take one or more written exams, including one administered by the Comprehensive Adult Student Assessment System to establish their English-language level and enable a smooth transition into unit programs. Lower-level students may proceed to sector-based contextualized classes (e.g., ESOL for healthcare jobs, bridge to technology jobs), funded under WIOA, to explore their career options while learning more English. Higher-level students ready to obtain a credential and interested in a MI-BEST class (e.g., certified apartment maintenance technician) meet with an interviewer who, using a rubric, screens for oral English level, career interest, employment goals, and readiness to engage in intensive coursework.

Nursing assistant candidates, for example, are asked about their experiences caring for others and their interest in working with people from different cultural backgrounds. Cut-off scores for written English-language assessments and oral interview questions are regularly recalibrated to align with data on student outcomes and expectations for entry-level employment. Basic English listening skills, for example, are required as nursing assistants must be able to follow health and safety directions. The interviewer collects all data into a spreadsheet for review by a selection committee that is responsible for ensuring that each candidate is treated equitably and that admission decisions are documented. In a final step, applicants review the program handbook and sign off, indicating their agreement to follow college policies on topics such as Title IX, FERPA, discipline concerns, sexual harassment, and program policies, particularly attendance and grading.

BUILDING A SERVICE DELIVERY MODEL

Over time, the college has come to see that there are certain core services needed to respond to the unique needs of immigrants for information, specialized instruction, and employment support. When tied to labor market needs, high-quality English-language instruction that focuses on workforce readiness and results in a labor market–recognized credential, paired with career navigation and job development services, can move people rapidly into entry-level employment.

Instruction

In choosing a sector area for program development, staff members engage in a deliberative process that considers a range of factors, not just quantitative employment data. Local salaries, student interests, community priorities, employer interest, and support from within the college discipline area all play a role. For example, certified apartment maintenance technicians are not on any top ten list of regional employment needs, but there are still more than enough jobs locally to match with the number of students served. In addition, these jobs may segue into other technical jobs, and the program enjoys significant employer support.

Scheduling for the courses is challenging. Contextualized sector-based classes for the lower-level students are typically offered in the evenings, as this is when the largest number of students are available. MI-BEST classes for higher-level learners require a serious commitment; they take place in the daytime, given the three hundred to three hundred and fifty hours of instruction that are involved in the MI-BEST model, and are best suited for students who are unemployed and need entry-level jobs.

A typical MI-BEST schedule includes four days a week of instruction. Half of each instruction day is spent with the two instructors coteaching the technical content and English. The other half of the day is spent on additional ESOL needs, workforce readiness, and other skill needs, such as math review. One day a week is reserved for students to meet with career navigators, job developers, or tutors; to work independently; or to take care of personal or family needs.

To mitigate some of the scheduling challenges, staff members have experimented with the number of hours of instruction to see if there is an ideal minimum; there is not. However, the expectation (and the foundation for budgeting) is about three hundred total hours: one hundred hours of content-based instruction jointly taught by technical content and ESOL instructors, one hundred hours of ESOL instruction, and an additional one hundred hours of "other instruction." This includes bridge instruction to cover vocabulary and review content background knowledge along with related reading and numeracy skills, clinical hours if required, tutoring, and test-taking practice toward the end of the course.

Support Services

Often immigrant students use the same strategies for finding work that they used in their countries of origin: they seek the help of friends and family. In the United States, however, friends and family may not have the same network of opportunities as in their first countries. Students are usually not aware of the federally funded workforce system, and it may not address their needs for more in-depth guidance. Supportive college and career services offered in the AEBSCC unit aim to fill this critical need for students.

College and career coaches are adjunct faculty who serve students enrolled in contextualized classes on-site with career information, job applications, interviewing skills, and information about transitioning to college. Career navigators work intensively with MI-BEST students from the beginning to address any social service needs that could affect participation, link students to social service agencies for ongoing assistance throughout the student's time in the course, develop individualized education and employment plans, and delve more deeply into career choices and educational opportunities through individual appointments and workshops. These services remain available to students after program completion as students implement career plans, enroll in their next coursework at the college, and sort out financial aid and scholarships.

Once students are approaching MI-BEST course completion, they meet with a job developer who will do more one-on-one employment work, target specific jobs for application, conduct outreach to employers to identify positions and needs, arrange for career fairs, and offer postemployment follow-up and retention services. At the same time, job developers are "selling" program students to meet the needs of employers, carefully presenting graduates as competent, well-trained, experienced candidates who will become valuable employees, not as clients learning English with extensive social service needs. The job developer thus advertises the program itself and the college as a whole, while reporting back to staff on successes and challenges and antici-pated needs.

STAFFING FOR SUCCESS

Regardless of staffing, certain core functions need to be covered in work-force ESOL programs. These are in direct response to the unique needs of immigrants and how they find education and employment. In the early days of MI-BEST, staff members tried bravely to cover all of these functions in their regular lines of duty, but it quickly became apparent that, given the new priorities on workforce education, dedicated staffing would be required if the program were to succeed.

Meeting students where they are, on days, evenings, and weekends is critically important, so the outreach coordinator (a full-time position funded over time with a variety of public and private funds) has deep ties to the local community along with a broad understanding of college programming and career opportunities. Grant funding has also provided the unit with a full-time MI-BEST instructor and curriculum developer who moves between the different projects, helping develop programs, implementing initial course-work, and training other adjunct instructors to follow.

Finally, the most recent additions to the AEBSCC unit employment ros-ters are the career navigators and job developers. These positions are a bit unusual in the community college environment, growing out of a long-ob-served need for services and a new reality where grant outcomes can mean anything from education to employment.

In the early days of the Refugee Training Program, boundaries between institutions were clear: educators did the teaching and some guidance and advising, and resettlement agencies did traditional job development and placement. With early employment as the priority in the national refugee resettlement system, job development for refugees included many of the services seen today: direct contact with employers on behalf of students; employment more personalized to a participant's background; and follow-up and retention services to support on-the-job success. This service delivery model clearly informed Montgomery College staff who worked on these projects over the years, leading to an expectation that all adult students both needed and deserved this level of service.

Consequently, over the years, the AEBSCC unit experimented with a variety of ways to provide these services, from referrals to nonprofits to partnering with local workforce agencies to subcontracting with agencies for a specific set of services. Partners tried to meet these needs, but often their understanding of career services was limited to basic advising, filling out a résumé, and workshops on interviewing skills—simply not the level of support immigrant clients need. For this and other reasons such as agency staffing turnover, these partnerships often did not result in the expected level of service to address grant funder requirements, and it became increasingly clear that there was a hole in the county's service capacity that was not going to be filled any time soon.

This led the AEBSCC unit at the college to include positions for career navigation and job development in every funding application, arguing that this supports both grant outcome requirements while meeting the college's mission of student success. Now other career navigator positions are emerging throughout the college as other units begin to understand the need for intensive career guidance and services for all students and how they can support program and college completion and success.

SUSTAINABILITY: LEVERAGING THE PAST
TO PLAN FOR THE FUTURE

Sustainability is a concern for any kind of program such as this. The AEBSCC unit has been exceptionally fortunate in obtaining funding for these programs and services, but strategic thinking has certainly played a role. From the early days of programming until now, unit staff members have intentionally leveraged past programming, services, and lessons learned to inform future projects. Sustainability planning also must encompass leveraging and cross-training of staff; this becomes critical as people leave the program for new opportunities and others join with fresh waves of energy and enthusiasm.

Pilot projects, such as the apartment maintenance program, were tested with more flexible money before moving to more restrictive funding with specific outcomes. Services, such as providing in-house scholarship money for additional coursework and outreach, were piloted with smaller groups of targeted students, to test and refine strategies before going mainstream. In turn, at each of these initial opportunities, a variety of data on student outcomes and services (e.g., wage gains and job developer caseloads) was collected that would help support future program requests and funding design.

Over time, these data points helped underpin funding requests as well as advocacy work. Advocacy has occurred on multiple levels both within the college and the local community. Over time, AEBSCC staff members have joined any number of college initiatives and governance groups, sharing information about programming and students with staff from the Montgomery College Foundation and with the college's legislative affairs office.

In turn, as these offices started to become more connected to programs and students, they looked for ways to help support the work. Foundation staff mentioned programming to outside funders and legislative staff members were helpful in linking AEBSCC staff to the Montgomery County Council, which provided further support. Sharing success stories with all of these offices helped everyone understand that they had a role to play in the success of the program's students. In addition, more than once, staff members have emphasized that effective policies and practices from workforce education models such as this can have a positive influence on a range of students, not just immigrants and refugees.

Finally, sustainability is supported by understanding that the college is the brand, and leveraging that brand brings huge opportunities. The college brand allows staff to form partnerships and networks that immigrant students simply do not have access to when they arrive. Given the size of the college, and the fact that it is fully accredited, staff can advocate and negotiate on behalf of students. For example, after making changes to nursing assistant curricula to include digital literacy skills, staff reminded employers of the value added in working with the college and advocated for raises for program graduates.

In another case, where hiring managers insisted employees had to have personal transportation to provide after-hours on-call services—an obvious barrier for students on public transportation—staff proposed that graduates could instead each have a college program-approved personal transportation plan that would include the student's commitment to having access to private transportation and cash always on hand to cover the ride. In turn, once given that access to the college's employment networks, students carry that brand with them to the world of work, allowing employers to further buy into and support the work.

LESSONS LEARNED

Although small in size, these programs are mighty in their effectiveness and capacity to positively affect the lives of immigrant and refugee students like Abdel and their families as they find their way in the United States. These programs should not, however, be the only time Montgomery College touches a family; the college's goal is to build a lifelong relationship with students that will have them and their family members returning over the years as their needs and goals evolve. Values underpin the work and partnerships support it. Meeting students where they are and offering services proven to work are key. Building programs that can evolve and grow over time, while demonstrating how they can support the community beyond immigrants and refugees, ensures a better future for everyone.

NOTES

1. "Stories of Success: I Am Proud," Greater Washington Workforce Development Collaborative of the Community Foundation for the National Capital Region, Washington, DC, http://gwwdc.org/program.

2. "Montgomery College Mission," Montgomery College, accessed July 23, 2018, https://www.montgomerycollege.edu/about-mc/mission-values.html.

3. Margie McHugh and Madeleine Morawski, *Immigrants and WIOA Services: Comparison of Sociodemographic Characteristics of Native and Foreign-Born Adults in Montgomery County, Maryland* (Washington, DC: Migration Policy Institute, 2016), 2, http://www.migrationpolicy.org/research/immigrants-and-wioa-services-comparison-sociodemographic-characteristics-native-and-foreign. See Table 1. Numbers have been rounded to the thousands and percentages to the whole.

4. McHugh and Morawski, *Immigrants and WIOA Services*, 5. See Table 3. Numbers have been rounded to the thousands and percentages to the whole.

5. Montgomery College Office of Institutional Research and Analysis, email message to author, June 20, 2018.

6. Montgomery College Office of Institutional Research and Analysis, email message to author, June 20, 2018.

7. Baltimore City Community College, Community Colleges of Baltimore County, Prince George's Community College, and Montgomery College were on this original team.

8. For a discussion of the I-BEST model, see John Wachen, Davis Jenkins, Clive Belfield, and Michelle Van Noy, *Contextualized College Transition Strategies for Adult Basic Skills Students: Learning from Washington State's I-BEST Program Model* (New York: Columbia University, December 2012), accessed May 4, 2018, http://ccrc.tc.columbia.edu/media/k2/attachments/i-best-program-final-phase-report.pdf.

9. Dominic Modicamore, Yvette Lamb, Jeffrey Taylor, Ama Takyi-Laryea, Kathy Karageorge, and Enzo Ferroggiaro, *Accelerating Connections to Employment, Vol. 1. Final Evaluation Report* (Baltimore: ICF and the Baltimore County Department of Economic and Workforce Development, May 1, 2017), accessed May 4, 2018, http://resources.baltimorecountymd.gov/Documents/EconomicDevel/acevolume1.pdf.

10. Modicamore et al., *Accelerating Connections to Employment*.

11. US Department of Education, *Program Memorandum OCTAE/DAEL 15-7* (Washington, DC: US Department of Education, January 2016), accessed August 1, 2018, https://www2.ed.gov/about/offices/list/ovae/pi/AdultEd/octae-program-memo-15-7-ielce.pdf.

12. US Department of Education and Manhattan Strategy Group, *Integrated Education and Training Guide, 34 CFR, Part 463, Subpart D: Building Opportunities through Integrated English Literacy and Civics Education* (Washington, DC: US Department of Education, n.d.), accessed August 1, 2018, https://lincs.ed.gov/sites/default/files/IET_checklist508FINAL_0.pdf.

Chapter Ten

Data-Driven Redesign Provides New Pathways to College and Careers

Cynthia Hatch

Like many community colleges around the United States, Northern Virginia Community College (NOVA) is home to students from many different backgrounds, countries, and stages of life. NOVA is the largest public educational institution in Virginia and the second-largest community college in the United States, with six campuses offering more than 160 associate degrees, certificate programs, distance learning, and workforce credentials. Serving students from more than 180 different countries, NOVA provides immigrant, international, and native-born students the opportunity to learn from each other while undertaking their academic or career certificate studies.

When immigrants arrive in the United States and look for work, they must learn new culture and workplace norms. Many also need assistance with their language skills. NOVA's Office of Workforce Development—known as NOVA Workforce—supports these students, as well as international students, through its American Culture and Language Institute (ACLI). ACLI is often immigrant students' first introduction to NOVA. As part of the NOVA Workforce, ACLI provides noncredit English as a second language (ESL) instruction to students from seventy-five countries at five NOVA campuses.

NOVA has a long tradition of providing college and career readiness support through a variety of programs. From its preacademic ESL programs (e.g., college ESL and ACLI) and college and career readiness initiatives (e.g., Training Futures, Pathway to the Baccalaureate, Adult Career Pathways, ESL for Employment, and Global Learning Center), immigrant students receive English-language instruction and career readiness training in an effort to break down barriers to college and careers.

To serve those students' educational and career needs, ACLI has implemented a part-time ESL program called Career Readiness, which offers workforce-contextualized English classes for students at high-beginning through intermediate ESL levels. In Career Readiness, students develop skills in work-related communication via case studies, such as participating in meetings, negotiations, and interviews; and writing emails, reports, and proposals. Students' soft skills in teamwork and intercultural communication are also developed via working-across-cultures units. Career counselors from NOVA Workforce visit Career Readiness classes to provide students with timely next steps to transition from ESL to workforce credentials classes.

The intent of this effort is to assist in transitioning part-time program students from contextualized ESL to sector-specific content instruction. Optional support-ESL classes such as grammar, pronunciation, and a learning lab provide supplementary, soft-skill instruction to promote students' persistence and prepare them for the workforce.

This chapter addresses NOVA's efforts, through a curriculum redesign process, to address the needs of its immigrant students and their aspirations to gain career readiness skills through English-language instruction. ACLI staff members have accelerated the use of data to evaluate, redesign, and tailor curriculum to improve training and target student and employer needs more effectively.

ACLI BACKGROUND AND GOALS

ACLI evolved out of noncredit ESL programs that NOVA established in the mid-1980s. These programs were operated independently at different campuses until 2009, when the college established a task force to coordinate all ESL programs and create a core set of noncredit courses to be taught on five NOVA campuses.

The institute's key goals are to (1) prepare students for successful transition into an associate degree or a workforce credentials program, (2) develop students' workforce and communication skills to become productive community members, (3) prepare students to move from lower- to higher-paying jobs, and (4) offer customized ESL training in collaboration with local businesses to develop their employees' language skills and improve their productivity.

ACLI comprises an intensive English program and a part-time program that provide instruction in the four language skills (reading, writing, speaking, and listening). ACLI also offers specialty courses in test preparation and current events for higher-level students. The intensive English program prepares local immigrant residents (long-time and recent arrivals) and international students for college-level classes and associate degrees. The part-time program prepares local students for future careers and improves their social skills in English.

ACLI has served more than 32,000 students since 2009. The average ACLI student spends two semesters in the program. As of spring 2017, the majority of ACLI's 1,274 students were local residents who emigrated from more than 75 countries. International F-1 visa students represented 27 percent of ACLI participants. Approximately 41 percent of ACLI students are enrolled full-time and are high school graduates seeking associate degrees from NOVA. The other 59 percent are enrolled part-time and are seeking to improve their workplace English skills or enter workforce credentials programs.

To lead a review and eventual program redesign, NOVA Workforce created a centralized staff position: the ESL and Teaching English as a Second Language (TESOL) program developer and instructional designer. This program developer served as a lead facilitator between ACLI program coordinators, ESL instructors, ESL students, and the NOVA Workforce leadership team throughout the development and implementation of the part-time program redesign and future curriculum development. The redesign process was conducted over a five-month period, beginning in late spring 2017 and ending in fall 2017, when the first cohort of ESL students accessed the newly redesigned Career Readiness program.

MULTIPLE PATHWAYS TO COLLEGE AND CAREERS

For the first time ESL students now have the opportunity to transition from contextualized ESL instruction to NOVA Workforce's credentials programs. In the Career Readiness program, immigrant students can elect to focus on one of NOVA Workforce's certificate pathways in information technology (IT), healthcare, or business via a small-group project, which consists of interviews with a NOVA workforce instructor, career counselor, or an employer about the skills and knowledge employees need to be successful in class and at work. In this way, students are informed on the steps needed to attain an industry credential and secure more opportunities and professional fulfillment in the US workplace.

Figure 10.1 illustrates the multiple entry and exit points for ACLI students in the redesigned part-time program. Each of the five levels takes approximately one hundred hours to complete during an academic year. Students may take part-time ESL classes at any of five different skill levels (low-beginning to intermediate) and either continue to college ESL or shift into Career Readiness classes (starting at the high-beginning level, level 3), which lead to workforce credentials courses in education, IT, healthcare, and business or management. Career Readiness classes provide a "reality check" so that students can be confident about their eventual workforce credentials choices.

Support-ESL classes for ACLI students usually begin two weeks after the part-time ESL and Career Readiness classes, and last for eight weeks. Support-ESL classes take twenty hours to complete. The multidirectional entry and exit points of the part-time program mean that immigrant students have the flexibility to adjust the context of their ESL instruction at each semester, and support can be provided to a wider audience than ESL students. Immigrant students already in workforce credentials courses, who would benefit from additional ESL support, can take the support-ESL courses to improve their grammar, pronunciation, and learning-technology skills.[1]

EXPLORING STUDENT MOTIVATIONS
FOR IMPROVING ENGLISH

Staff and administrators in the ACLI use the results of regularly administered (midterm, end-of-term, and annual) student surveys to evaluate program outcomes and guide any program changes. This process was followed to redesign the part-time program in 2017, which now includes pathways between part-time ESL and workforce credentials programs. ACLI's surveys were initially conducted in person and on paper; later surveys were conducted online via an email link sent to students and facilitated by ESL instructors. The involvement of instructors in surveying students, such as taking students

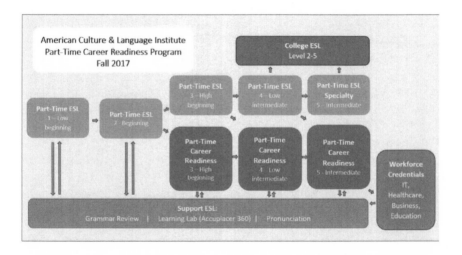

Figure 10.1.   Part-Time ESL Career Readiness Program. Reprinted with permission of Northern Virginia Community College.

to a computer lab to complete the online surveys, led to higher response rates for both in-person and online surveys.

A key data point that influenced the program redesign came from survey questions asking students about their current employment and their future career aspirations. Survey results in both fall 2016 and spring 2017 showed a distinct trend for students currently employed in low-paying jobs (e.g., childcare, food service) wanting to move into high-paying, high-demand jobs (e.g., IT, healthcare, business).

Surveys of 583 current and former students in June 2016 and May 2017 indicated that 83 percent of ACLI students took classes to improve their English skills. Furthermore, 82 percent said ACLI classes "very much" or "somewhat" helped them meet their goals, 78 percent were "very" or "somewhat" satisfied with their experience at ACLI, and 70 percent of students were working either full- or part-time after completing ACLI.

In response to an additional question on the May 2017 survey, sixty-four students reported their current occupations and future career aspirations. Thirty-eight percent were employed in low-paying jobs (customer service, childcare, or food service) and 18 percent were employed in high-paying jobs (business, IT, healthcare, or education). Only 6 percent wanted to continue working in customer service, childcare, or food service in the next five years, while 71 percent wanted to have jobs in business, IT, healthcare, or education in the next five years.

Another key finding of the student surveys was that the traditional progression from ESL to an associate degree at NOVA was not the main motivator for many immigrant residents. Eighty percent of students reported obtaining a college degree in their home countries before attending NOVA. Prior education meant that most immigrant students reported they were motivated to take ESL by a desire to enter the US labor force or transition from lower-paying jobs to higher-paying, high-demand jobs in the northern Virginia region in many of the same high-demand career sectors for which NOVA Workforce offered training. Employers in these same sectors, especially information technology, often struggle to find qualified candidates who can speak and write in English.[2]

LEARNING FROM OTHER LEADERS

In addition to surveying student needs, ACLI staff researched various noncredit workforce-contextualized ESL programs at community colleges and community-based organizations across the country. Staff also consulted two sources—the *College and Career Readiness Standards for Adult Education* (CCR)[3] and the *English Language Proficiency Standards for Adult Education* (ELP)[4]—to determine the degree to which adult basic education and

ESL programs in the United States addressed the instructional shifts from life skills to work skills outlined in the standards.

Yet, although the programs ACLI reviewed for the redesign aligned with the CCR and ELP guidelines, ACLI staff learned that a common challenge reported by these program coordinators following redesign was changing students' perceptions of the type of ESL instruction they needed. Many students were not aware of the potential benefits of workforce-contextualized English instruction for their current and future careers, and often requested a general English class. This was an essential learning point for ACLI program coordinators, who made sure that additional student counseling would be available to ensure students understood the new Career Readiness option and would enroll in classes that best match their goals and interests. To address this advising issue prior to implementation, ACLI staff visited part-time ESL classrooms to brief students about the new program and planned additional student advising for the fall 2017 semester.

ACLI's new pathway was clear. A workforce-contextualized ESL program could transition more students into workforce-credentials courses in IT, healthcare, and business, thereby creating a pipeline of trained entry- to mid-level candidates for northern Virginia area companies.

CHALLENGES

The largest challenge facing NOVA's international and immigrant students is the fact that ACLI is a self-funded program through student tuition. These students cannot use Pell Grants or other financial aid to pay for ACLI ESL classes. In an effort to remain affordable, ACLI has kept tuition increases to a minimum and remains competitive with other community college–based ESL programs. However, if NOVA could secure grant funding for ESL students—which it seeks occasionally—it would improve student outcomes by allowing the continuation of their studies.

A secondary challenge facing international and resident students at NOVA is the perceived duplication of ESL programs at the college. Although ACLI acts as a feeder program into college ESL, a lack of sequential-level identification across both programs often confuses prospective students. NOVA has expedited the transition between the two programs through the use of a bridge writing exam. ACLI also implemented a college-wide placement test of writing, speaking, and listening, and college-wide objective statements for each ACLI level.

Finally, with lower enrollment trends generally, it made sense to consolidate offerings, focusing on classes that met immigrant students' goals for their English-language instruction. An integrated skills approach—in which students received instruction in speaking, listening, reading, and writing in one class, instead of paying for two classes of paired skills—was predicted to greatly reduce students' tuition and textbook costs.

STRATEGIES FOR SUCCESSFUL IMPLEMENTATION

Key to any curriculum redesign is getting adequate stakeholder buy-in by communicating the new direction and the reasons for the new direction in a timely manner.[5] Additionally, providing preplanned phases for stakeholders to give feedback on the curriculum, assessments, and textbooks is important for a curriculum redesign success.

An important step in the redesign was to develop a timeline to incorporate rounds of feedback and revision, which started in the summer of 2017. The review process initially included ACLI program coordinators, who also serve as campus-based ESL instructional experts. Once the program coordinators approved the new part-time Career Readiness program, the ESL and TESOL program developer briefed NOVA Workforce management and operations staff and ACLI instructors through a series of web-based presentations that allowed synchronous discussions with large numbers of staff and instructors dispersed across NOVA's five campuses.

Stakeholder buy-in was boosted by creating an advising plan for existing ESL students and by adapting existing ACLI assessment tools, including a rubric and departmental exams to evaluate student progress across four skills during the fall 2017 semester. Keeping tuition costs low for students as well as student unfamiliarity with computers meant that ACLI did not adopt the use of computerized placement tests. The postprogram assessment involved all stakeholders, including students, instructors, and ACLI coordinators.

Consolidating the part-time program's textbook series from more than twenty down to two removed various barriers for students, including multiple textbook purchases and a lack of collaboration between part-time instructors resulting from their use of different materials.

ACLI provides professional development and opportunities for instructor collaboration through its Teacher Appreciation Day mini conferences and "What Works" seminars at certain campuses each year. The part-time program redesign enabled greater levels of collaboration for instructors who were now using the same materials and the same assessment tools.

Internal partnerships across NOVA's campuses are critical to ACLI's success, and there are several efforts to improve the transition of ACLI students into college-level programs. Staff in the for-credit college ESL program help ACLI students advance by evaluating exit-level intensive English program students' readiness to enter the college ESL program, via the Accuplacer exam and the bridge writing exam. NOVA Workforce's student success advisors provide career and college advising for ACLI students interested in pursuing credit or noncredit workforce-credentials programs.

Finally, also important to ACLI's success is the number of external partners—such as local literacy councils, public schools, and nonprofit organizations—that regularly refer ESL students to ACLI to continue to study English or enter college ESL. International entities such as the Saudi Arabian Cultural Mission and universities in Turkey and Brazil have provided funding for student scholarships and faculty professional development.

DATA-DRIVEN PROGRAM REFINEMENT: LOOKING TOWARD THE FUTURE

Midway through the fall 2017 semester, ACLI surveyed its instructors and students to determine levels of satisfaction with the new curriculum, the textbooks, and the assessments. Students and instructors were surveyed separately using an online platform.

Most instructors felt they were given the necessary program overview and materials to teach. Additionally, instructors felt that students were placed well and were able to meet the course objectives. The majority of instructors requested additional professional development, including more norming and opportunities for peer-to-peer collaboration.

All part-time students in both ESL and Career Readiness courses were surveyed. High student satisfaction with the new programs confirmed that the redesign better met their needs for English instruction. Approximately 81 percent of the 187 students reported that they were satisfied and felt that their English was improving. Students were also asked for suggestions to improve their courses. More speaking and a greater variety of activities were the most requested improvements at approximately 22 percent and 15 percent respectively. Part-time students also requested that more time be added to the fifty hours of instruction each semester.

LESSONS LEARNED

Change in the context of a large division like NOVA Workforce has been likened to turning a very big ship. More than one hundred NOVA Workforce staff and six hundred students were engaged in the change process. By engaging ACLI program coordinators' content expertise, ten new courses and accompanying assessments were developed and approved in a five-month period. Training instructors and NOVA Workforce staff using online tools enabled the same information to be shared with all stakeholders in a timely manner. Online surveys of instructors and students during and at the end of the semester provided opportunities for issues to be addressed. Finally, a major lesson learned has been accepting that not all stakeholders will embrace change, but that change will still occur.

Change is growing at NOVA today. By the end of the academic 2017–2018 year, nearly one hundred immigrant students had enrolled in Career Readiness classes. In spring 2018, improved student advising and word of mouth led to 64 percent of Career Readiness enrollment coming from new student registration and 34 percent from students transitioning out of the part-time ESL program.

Steven B. Partridge, NOVA Workforce vice president, noted,

> The life cycle of educational programs is getting shorter; therefore educational institutions must constantly redesign our offerings to meet the needs of today's diverse workforce. To ensure we develop the skills demanded by employers, we must be intentional in creating meaningful training for students and employers, while also ensuring any training we offer is both stackable and has a clear path to real-world employment opportunities. With NOVA Workforce's Career Readiness program, for the first time, English-language learners can transition from contextualized ESL instruction to workforce credentials programs, thereby providing students with a pathway to earn credentials in Northern Virginia's high-demand sectors.

NOTES

1. As defined by David H. Jonassen, "Learning technology is any environment or definable set of activities that engages learners in knowledge construction and meaning-making." For further information, see David H. Jonassen, "Supporting Communities of Learners with Technology: A Vision for Integrating Technology with Learning in Schools," *Educational Technology* 35, no. 4 (1995): 60–63.

2. *Survey: Qualified Workers Are Harder to Find* (Alexandria, VA: Society for Human Resource Management, 2016).

3. Susan Pimentel, *College and Career Readiness Standards for Adult Education* (Washington, DC: US Department of Education, Office of Vocational and Adult Education, 2013), https://lincs.ed.gov/publications/pdf/CCRStandardsAdultEd.pdf.

4. American Institutes for Research, *English Language Proficiency Standards for Adult Education* (Washington, DC: US Department of Education, Office of Vocational and Adult Education, 2016), https://lincs.ed.gov/publications/pdf/elp-standards-adult-ed.pdf.

5. Michael Carroll, "From Curriculum Design to Implementation," in *Developing a New Curriculum for Adult Learners* (Alexandria, VA: TESOL International Press, 2007), 22.

Reflective Narrative

We Are Not All the Same—Listening to Concerns of Beginning English-Language Learners

Heide Spruck Wrigley

Many of the chapters in this book highlight the key program features that support the persistence and success of students preparing for career pathway programs. These include comprehensive case management, proactive counseling, student-centered advising, and meaningful collaboration among stakeholders. This reflective narrative seeks to present characteristics of quality programs from the perspective of beginning nontraditional English-language learners who are participating or would like to participate in career pathway programs. These suggestions are based on my professional work interviewing students, observing classes, and providing technical assistance to a wide range of programs, including those at community colleges, adult schools, and community-based organizations.

Here, then, is a compilation of voices that have emerged through one-on-one and small-group interactions with students from programs across the United States.

DIVERSE BACKGROUNDS, DIVERSE NEEDS

All of the students who have talked with me as part of these programs have been foreign-born. Some were long-term residents of the United States living in neighborhoods where daily life (e.g., shopping, going to a clinic, talking to social services) can be negotiated without speaking much English. These students tend to have a fairly high English recognition vocabulary[1] and often have a good sense of how the systems they have used work (e.g., transportation, clinics, shopping). Many are women who have raised children and run households. Many have sound math skills, having been in charge of the family budget. Yet they may doubt their own abilities to succeed in an academic or training class, often feeling they are too old to learn.

Discovering and building on the wealth of experience in planning and executing tasks and working with others to get things done is a real strength of this group. Providing established residents with opportunities to guide newcomers through joint projects (such as community mapping) can let their survival skills shine and builds the confidence that comes from working collaboratively to accomplish tasks that may appear daunting to an individual.

On the other end of the spectrum I have met those who are relatively new to the United States—many of them refugees—who need to learn about educational norms and systems while still developing their language skills. Too much information about career pathway options, provided all at once in orientation sessions, becomes overwhelming. Many newcomers talk about information overload and feeling embarrassed when they missed key points, only to hear an instructor say, "But we explained this in our first session." Offering key information in chunks, repeating critical points often, offering fact sheets in translation, and inviting local community-based organizations (CBOs) to help deliver workshops to heighten cross-cultural skills for students and staff can go a long way in building community across agencies and decreasing the social isolation of newcomer students.

FAMILY INVOLVEMENT

In the United States, we tend to see the locus of decision-making in the individual. We ask students to tell us about plans and goals and then, as counselors, work with them one-on-one. Yet for many refugee and immigrant families, decisions are made by the family, with the individual student only one of the voices. Economic circumstances, work traditions, family needs, and gender roles all might influence the plans for a career. Having one member of a family take time out from work to attend an intensive program can mean fewer resources—money, time, childcare—available to the rest of the family.

When these issues are not thoroughly discussed and considered by the family, the success of a student may be inhibited and an individual may end up in a career track for which they have little enthusiasm, resulting in disappointment and high dropout rates. I have heard a number of students say, "My parents wanted me to study accounting, but I hate it."

Working with schools, places of worship, or CBOs to invite families to an outreach session where they can ask questions and then give everyone time to explore available options (including requirements for financial aid) can help families make informed decisions that take their personal realities into account. A facilitator can explain pros and cons of a particular route to be taken: a strong initial investment in time and resources can result in higher wages in the end—wages that can contribute significantly to a family's income. I have often seen families who, after gaining more knowledge and having thoughtful discussions with staff, decided to invest in a family member and support them through a career in the trades that they initially had rejected as taking too long or being inappropriate, particularly for young women.

HONORING AND SHARING STORIES

We all have stories that are uniquely our own. All students have life experiences, thoughts, and dreams that shape their expectations for themselves and their vision of the future. Even the most telling stories are not easily captured in surveys, demographic inventories, or needs assessments. Although giving a broad overview of particular groups, these documents miss many important nuances. They don't tell us that a woman has seen a family member shot and another heard of a friend being tortured. They don't capture trauma that makes it difficult to concentrate as images of violence flash through a student's mind. If we do not listen to and share students' stories, we miss opportunities to build empathy for immigrants and refugees, not only in our programs but also in the wider community.

The stories we miss need not be accounts of despair, fear, and violence; they may include past achievements to which we are oblivious. For example, many students have held important positions in their villages or towns. They were highly respected and a source of advice that others were eager to hear. Yet most of us do not ask deeper questions about the many different roles that students have played in their lives.

It is difficult for those outside the community to imagine how deeply loss of status can affect a person's social identity. Time and time again I have heard refugees say or imply, "I used to be somebody and now I am just someone with an accent who doesn't understand how things work." Inviting students to tell us about their daily lives and the work they did (formal or informal) and to share the story with others who understand the importance of these roles can help uplift students and connect them with each other. Storytelling that allows work-related skills and experiences to merge can easily take place in English as a second language (ESL) classes. These accounts can be shared not just with counselors, but with technical faculty who may have fewer opportunities to interact with nontraditional learners from other countries.

Stories can also provide details about the many turbulent factors in students' lives that make persistence and success so difficult for those who face challenging circumstances daily. In some programs these details are captured in formal ways as part of comprehensive case management.[2]

THE BILINGUAL BRAIN

By definition, students becoming proficient in another language have two linguistic systems to draw on. Both systems interact and can serve to facilitate learning. Yet too often, we treat English as the only language that counts and fail to show students how to use all their linguistic resources to process information and learn. We know from brain research that bilingual students cannot help translating when they encounter difficulties in new languages. Telling these students, "Think in English; don't translate," is of little use as the brain automatically seeks equivalencies in the languages it has available. Encouraging students to take advantage of occasional translation support can reduce frustration and speed up the learning process, as the meaning of a new concept will be revealed more rapidly through a quick translation than a potentially confusing and lengthy explanation in English.

Bilingual adults have spoken to me at length about the help they need so they can keep up with their English-speaking peers. They appreciate that classes are held in English and are aware that constant translation robs them of the opportunity to let English sink in and take hold. Many students wish academic or technical instructors would share their lecture outlines and key vocabulary ahead of the class, so that they can prepare their minds for what is to come and look up unfamiliar words and phrases (including pronunciation) ahead of time. Yet this seldom happens.

Most appreciated are instructors who have clear outlines of the points they will be making in their lectures and match their outlines to the headings and sequence of topics in the textbook chapters assigned for additional reading. Students are often disappointed and frustrated when technical instructors do not recognize how long it takes them to make it through a textbook chapter just reading the words, let alone absorb and understand the information. Most English-language learners read fairly slowly and many spend hours looking up vocabulary they are not sure about, never reaching the end of a chapter. Showing these students how to navigate a textbook effectively and encouraging them to form study circles to discuss key points to remember and prepare for tests can go a long way in evening the playing field for those who have to learn in a language they still don't fully understand. Time-worn strategies used by the rest of us—such as scanning the first and last paragraphs of a chapter before reading the main text and skipping sidebars when under time pressure—could be shared with students who are so overwhelmed by the sheer number of unknown words in a textbook that they give up.

MAKING ACHIEVEMENTS VISIBLE

The achievement of hands-on technical skills is often easy to see. We can observe a student taking a patient's blood pressure or hear the student explain how to change a filter in an air-conditioning unit. Improvements in language and literacy are more difficult to capture and students often feel they are not making much progress, lamenting, "I've taken all these ESL classes and I still don't speak English"—a sentiment sometimes reinforced by attitudes of less-sensitive instructors. I am often surprised when asking students, "What can you now do in English that you could not do before this class," and seeing them stymied by the question. They might recite what they studied (e.g., present tense, the parts of a car engine, or the history of tuberculosis) but only a few students are able to explain what they can get done using English (e.g., describe the jobs people in their family have had; deconstruct a medicine label; install and run free virus software on a computer; give a bed bath to a homebound patient)

Students get tested with increasing frequency, and while standardized tests can provide important information on overall proficiency levels, they often fail to capture how well a student can get a point across in English in spite of limited skills, or demonstrate information a student can understand when key concepts are related to a field in which they have some experience. Also needed are assessments that show students what they can do to make learning visible and help them recognize the progress they are making. For example, "Can Do" lists, coupled with demonstrations of skills or other competency-based assessments, can go a long way in showing both students and instructors which skills have been acquired and which need to be developed. While these types of assessments are quite common in skills-based technical classes, they could also be created for language classes that prepare students for work or training.

Case in point: OneAmerica's national English Innovations[3] project—a set of community-based programs[4] that serve as on-ramps to more formal education in colleges or adult education schools—has long used "Can Do" lists to have students identify the English and technology skills they are comfortable using, as well as those that still present challenges. Students use a checklist with a scale to indicate how competent they feel in a certain area (e.g., using Google maps to find the fastest way to the employment office, or filling out a job application on paper or online[5]). After students fill in individual charts, they work in groups to demonstrate to others what they can do well and get help with the skills in which they do not yet feel competent.

Students also get a chance to respond to the class at the end of each unit. They fill in exit cards (also known as "ticket out the door"), writing down one important idea or skill they learned, one concept that they still find confusing, and one question they still have. Sometimes they simply provide open-ended feedback on how they are feeling in class, what they enjoy, and what frustrates them. They also offer suggestions on how to improve the learning experience for themselves and others.

IMPLICATIONS FOR CAREER NAVIGATORS

Both in my private life living close to the US–Mexico border and my professional life working with programs serving immigrants and refugees with limited or interrupted schooling, I meet many adults who have not had a chance to think about career options, let alone pathways. Most are primarily focused on getting work, hoping for a good job (replacing multiple part-time jobs) or advancing in a current job. A fair number are stuck in entry-level positions that turn out to be dead-end jobs, and unless they get a chance to improve both their English proficiency and their level of technical skills, they will find it hard to obtain a job that offers wages that can lift a family out of poverty.

Career navigators can play an important role in helping these adults consider realistic options that take their current circumstances into account but also offer the possibility of significant change. Navigators can help identify hidden aspirations of adults who may have never thought about college. Meaningful advisement of nontraditional students new to the whole concept of certificates and career pathways takes time. Discussions need to be mindful of a family's financial situation and the commitments each member has. If vulnerable students are to recognize and take advantage of new opportunities, dialogue must be ongoing, hesitations need to be explored, and barriers must be identified so programmatic responses can be discussed by navigators and advisors. Building a relationship of trust is especially important if families are asked to make the investment in time and money that is required if a student is to persist beyond a first-level certificate.

Telling students about available options and advising them which courses to take is often sufficient for those with more traditional backgrounds, but is seldom enough for those facing difficult circumstances and doubting their own ability to succeed. If the process of deliberation is cut short, there is a risk that students will drop out because the pathway they selected is too challenging or is simply not the right fit.

Other considerations are important as well. I have been fortunate to talk to career counselors and navigators (several of them at South Texas College) who have spent time building trusting relationships with students, while at the same time setting high expectations and offering high levels of support. Here are a few tips based on those conversations:

Find commonalties between the work students have done and new opportunities. Many nontraditional students have worked in construction, farming, or landscaping; others may have taken care of relatives who have been homebound or have had long-term illnesses. Take note of informal skills when creating a profile for each person that contains not only data required by funders, but captures nonmeasurable experiences. Invite students to share their stories with the community. Give students a chance to tell details about their lives using drawings, storyboards, or photographs, and share these with local networks. Don't rely solely on print: Bring in an assortment of tools and instruments from various trades and invite students to demonstrate which ones they can use and which they would like to learn more about.

Explore students' interest in technical reading and other academic forms of learning. Ask if students have liked school in the past and whether they enjoyed books. Find out if they prefer hands-on labs to lectures, but explain that even trades courses generally have a lecture component. To assess reading interest and abilities, bring in trade books and journals written at various levels and ask students which materials they could easily understand and which they find challenging. For students not yet proficient in English, set up workshops focused on learning "how to learn." Demonstrate strategies for remembering information right after class (most students with ESL backgrounds find it difficult to listen for meaning and take notes at the same time), stress the importance of creating and studying personalized vocabulary lists, and offer tips on managing lengthy textbook assignments.

Be honest about the investment required by individuals or their families. Discuss the cost, time, and dispositions required to get a certificate and advance along the career ladder. Be upfront about cost outlays for mandatory purchasing such as uniforms or tools. Invite students to think about how they might afford ongoing training. Show the wages a person can earn at the different levels of the career ladder and help families who struggle see the long-term financial gains that might accrue if resources are pooled to support a person with a dream and the ambition to make it real. Tell the truth about Pell Grants and the dire consequences of dropping out of a course while receiving federal financial aid.[6]

Encourage women to consider nontraditional jobs and allow for conversations about challenges to expect in training or at the work site. Invite women who participated in classes with mostly men or worked at male-dominated sites to share both their experiences and the strategies they used to hold their own. Be positive but don't sugarcoat the issues. Discuss sexual harassment—what it is, how to avoid it, and how to file a complaint. Invite women to discuss if they ever filed or would file a complaint, what happened, and what results have been or might be. Stress the importance of building solidarity with other women who might have been harassed and filing complaints as a group, while recognizing that many women in lower-skilled jobs would not dream of filing a complaint against a supervisor, fearing repercussions.

Invite students to learn independently to get to know the language of their field. Show students where to find materials written at lower levels of English, such as high school textbooks or journals written for a general audience (e.g., magazines such as *Popular Mechanics* and *Health* or practical guides on topics such as home construction). Show students how to increase their knowledge and skills watching YouTube how-to videos and help them list vocabulary related to their field. Demonstrate how to use Google Translate to access the pronunciation of difficult words and phrases and highlight the advantage of personalized learning to supplement required course materials.

CONCLUSION

None of these ideas is necessarily new to those in the field who have been involved in programs preparing immigrants and refugees for work and careers. We have long known that nontraditional students with ESL backgrounds need a great deal of support to succeed and persist in technical or academic programs. We know that if learning is to be accelerated for vulnerable groups, support needs to be provided, circumstances need to be assessed, and case management needs to be in place. Yet we do not often take the time to truly get to know the students we plan to serve so we can design appropriate programs. Collaborating with other immigrant-serving agencies that know the community well can only strengthen our efforts. Listening to students, validating their experience, and honoring their stories is not just the right thing to do if we are educators. It is the first step in building program designs responsive to those who never before saw themselves as "college material."

NOTES

1. *English recognition vocabulary* refers to the set of words an individual recognizes, but does not know how to use correctly or consistently.

2. One example of a comprehensive assessment is the Family Development Matrix, a chart used in many community development programs in California, to identify where a family might fall on a continuum of indicators that range from "in crisis" to "thriving" (see https://csumb.edu/iccs/family-development-matrix-0) in areas such as housing, employment, literacy, and social-emotional health.

3. "English Innovations," One America, accessed November 1, 2018, https://weareoneamerica.org/what-we-do/programs/english-innovations.

4. Heide Wrigley, "English Innovations: Learning English with Digital Literacy and Community Engagement," Ed Tech Center, World Education, December 12, 2017, https://ed-tech.worlded.org/english-innovations.

5. Some companies allow applicants to download and print the online application for additional practice. See https://www.job-applications.com/mcdonalds-application-pdf.

6. If a student stops going to classes and effectively drops out or falls below full-time status, the student may be liable for repaying a portion of the Pell Grant received. See https://budgeting.thenest.com/pell-grant-need-paid-back-drop-out-33649.html.

Conclusion

A Roadmap for the Future — Reflections and Recommendations for Action

Jill Casner-Lotto

"Now more than ever we need to enlist other leading community colleges in our cause to support a multicultural and diverse student body that is vital for the economic, social, and cultural vibrancy of our communities and our country as well."—Belinda S. Miles, president, Westchester Community College

With those words, President Miles helped launch the Presidents for New American Success Pledge, the Community College Consortium for Immigrant Education's (CCCIE) national campaign to expand our network and engage community college presidents in CCCIE's work. The Presidents Pledge recognizes the direct correlation between immigrant and refugee integration and more vibrant communities where *all* Americans—newcomers and native-born residents alike—thrive.

College presidents who sign onto the pledge agree to support actions relating to five underlying principles: (1) demonstrating executive-level commitment by articulating a clear vision and strategy for supporting immigrant and refugee integration and allocating resources to make it happen, (2) developing frontline teams to bridge noncredit and credit programs and increase academic and career pathway opportunities, (3) using data-driven strategies to improve immigrant and refugee education and workforce development programs and services, (4) leveraging multisector partnerships to advance the success of immigrant and refugee students, and (5) replicating and scaling promising practices.

Compiling the case studies for this book and the companion book, *Working Together: How Community Colleges and Their Partners Help Immi-*

grants Succeed, has allowed CCCIE and its members to share our knowledge and experiences to build diverse campuses and communities, as well as provide a valuable opportunity to reflect on the progress and pitfalls along the way. The promising practices demonstrate how colleges are developing innovative initiatives to support immigrants and refugees that are integral to the mission of community colleges and contribute to the economic and social vitality of local communities and the country. And, although there is no "one-size-fits-all" approach to the design of initiatives supporting immigrant and refugee students, some valuable lessons emerge, suggesting a roadmap for the future.

In the hopes of stimulating a wider conversation at your college and in your community, here are several recommendations for actions, both drawn from books and gleaned directly from our authors' and member colleges' promising practices and lessons learned, and organized according to the principles of CCCIE's Presidents Pledge.

DEMONSTRATING EXECUTIVE COMMITMENT

Community college leaders are strong advocates for programs supporting immigrants and refugees. They bring together the resources that allow programs to succeed; facilitate participation at all levels of the college organization, from faculty to counselors to administrators, and across credit and noncredit departments; and engage with a variety of community stakeholders. They demonstrate a commitment to serving immigrants and refugees, by embedding diversity plans into college processes, emphasizing the economic and social justice imperatives, through both their words and actions. The role of leadership is articulated and expressed in college CEO's own words in Part I of this book; the influence—the demonstration of their commitment—is illustrated throughout, in all the chapters in both books. The following are some strategies to explore:

• Incorporate immigrant and refugee education initiatives into the college's strategic plan, and use data to monitor progress in these programs and services. Ensure that initiatives align with state-level high school and college completion goals and address current and projected skills shortages.
• Strengthen targeted immigrant and refugee education initiatives by leveraging academic and career support resources that are part of mainstream college completion, guided pathway, career pathway, and workforce development strategies serving a range of underrepresented, nontraditional students.
• Establish an immigrant and refugee resource center or a centralized point of contact to increase students' access to programs and services, and facil-

itate the necessary communications and connections with other college services, including admissions, financial aid, student support, and workforce development.

- Elevate the college's message of support for immigrant and refugee students—including Dreamers, Deferred Action for Childhood Arrivals (DACA) recipients, Temporary Protected Status (TPS) recipients, and all undocumented students—by reaffirming the college's commitment to diversity, inclusiveness, and equity as core values. Establish campus-wide, cross-departmental advisory teams comprising administrators, faculty, students, and staff to coordinate outreach and advocacy; provide training to frontline staff and faculty; and mobilize vital legal, financial, mental health, and other community resources.

- Advocate at the federal level for passage of a bipartisan Dream and Promise Act, providing a pathway to citizenship for Dreamers, including DACA recipients, those with TPS, and Deferred Enforced Departure (DED) holders. At the state level, advocate for extending access to in-state tuition, financial aid, drivers' licenses, and professional licensure to undocumented residents.

- Advocate for passage of the federal bipartisan Jobs Act that would extend Pell Grants to working students enrolled in quality short-term training programs leading to industry-recognized credentials in high-demand fields.

DEVELOPING FRONTLINE TEAMS AND BRIDGING CREDIT–NONCREDIT DIVIDES

Community colleges are engaging immigrant and refugee students, including prospective students, at much earlier stages to help them make informed choices about their educational and career options, develop individualized plans, and navigate the college to fulfill their intended goals. For students to better understand the full array of options available to them, frontline academic, continuing education, and workforce development advisors must be well versed in the college's programs on both the credit and noncredit sides. The development of English as a second language (ESL) bridge programs and short-term, stackable credentials that are part of career pathways require faculty and program developers to work across college divisions. The effectiveness of these models also depends on close coordination among academic, student services, adult education, and workforce development departments to facilitate immigrant and refugee students' transition into college degree or certificate programs that addresses their goals, whether on the credit or noncredit side of the house.

- Implement comprehensive outreach, intake, and assessment processes. Structure several outreach and intake sessions over time, focus initially on broad career sectors, and invite families to attend so they are involved in important decisions concerning childcare, transportation, and work schedules.
- Supplement standardized tests with additional assessment approaches to determine English language proficiency, address cultural differences, take into account students' foreign educational credentials and work experience, and capture the full picture of students' unique strengths and needs. Leverage existing programs and services in new ways, for example, through prior-learning assessments that can help students facing challenges in credential evaluation maximize their academic credits.
- Incorporate case management and college and career navigation services upon entry to ESL programs, and build internal credit–noncredit partnerships to break down silos across the college, strengthen counseling services, design curricula, and promote more seamless transitions to credit academic and career pathway programs.
- Provide immigrant college and career navigators who can offer guidance on job readiness and college knowledge that is unique or more complex for immigrants and refugees.
- Design differentiated ESL programs and pathways that recognize the unique strengths and needs of immigrant and refugee students at various educational and skill levels, including lower-educated adult learners who may lack high school diplomas, as well as foreign-educated immigrants and refugees seeking professional opportunities.
- Explore use of the Ability to Benefit financial aid provision to facilitate co-enrollment of immigrant students without a high school diploma or general equivalency diploma in credit postsecondary occupational credential programs while also acquiring basic literacy and ESL skills.
- Build pathways integrating ESL with academic and career preparation; quality short-term, industry-recognized credentials; and critical wraparound supports, such as financial aid, childcare, and transportation. Incorporate ESL on-ramps or bridge programs using contextualized curriculum.
- Empower students as peer mentors, program ambassadors, advocates, and community leaders. Invite immigrant and refugee students to speak at campus- and community-wide forums to share their experiences, challenges, and recommendations. Provide opportunities for students to share their expertise and help one another in the classroom as peer mentors and tutors and as role models in the community.
- Partner with community organizations to offer volunteer, service learning, and internship opportunities allowing students to develop leadership and advocacy skills, become civically engaged in their communities, and become better prepared to enter the workforce.

- Share student stories to convey the influence and importance of immigrant and refugee education and workforce development programs and build collaborative networks on and off campus.

USING DATA-DRIVEN STRATEGIES

Community colleges have not systematically gathered and disaggregated data on the educational and work backgrounds of their immigrant and refugee student populations or monitored their progress according to key performance indicators. Keeping track of employment outcomes can be especially difficult because they may be based on student self-report. Moreover, tracking outcomes as immigrants move between adult education, community college, community organization, and workforce development systems becomes challenging if there is no coordinated investment or effort to share data across these systems. However, some colleges are collecting data on students' background and progress, and using data to improve, expand, and sustain immigrant education programs and community outreach services.

- Conduct a community-wide needs analysis to capture labor market information, demographics, and specific immigration trends that enable the college to respond through effective program design, curriculum development, and outreach.
- Align the college's efforts with the local workforce development board, use data from the state employment department to identify trends in occupations and industries, and illustrate how immigrants and refugees can help address local, regional, and statewide skills shortages.
- Convene a cross-departmental data metrics working group at the college to explore barriers faced by immigrant and refugee students, along with ways to gather and use data to design differentiated ESL academic and career pathway programs and targeted interventions in case management and career counseling.
- Leverage any regional and national affiliations focused on strengthening performance outcomes and apply evidence-based practices and knowledge to programs serving immigrant and refugee student populations.

LEVERAGING THE POWER OF PARTNERSHIPS

Whether operating on a local community level or broader regional and state levels, multisector partnerships have proven essential for increasing immigrant and refugee students' transitions to further education, training, and employment, as well as integration into the social fabric of their communities. Community colleges collaborate with a variety of key stakeholders, including K–12 and four-year institutions; adult education systems; immigrant-serving community and faith-based organizations; national and local community foundations; individual employers and employer associations; national immigrant networks; federal, state, and municipal agencies; and workforce development boards.

- Build capacity, trust, and flexibility by cultivating relationships among various stakeholder groups. Capacity building includes partnership training, policy guidance, adequate funding, and investment in regional and statewide cross-sector data systems.
- Leverage complementary strengths and resources among partners on and off campus and look for opportunities for increased data sharing and joint advocacy directed at policymakers.
- Work closely with K–12 counselors and community leaders to inform immigrant students, including undocumented students, of dual-credit and early college high school options as a no-cost or low-cost way to accelerate degree completion and navigate career pathways.
- Tap into and align with state-level multisector workforce development partnerships to develop targeted approaches supporting skilled immigrants and refugees that alleviate acute labor shortages.
- Engage employers to identify skills gaps and workforce needs, review curriculum, and help design and support career pathways and training opportunities. Encourage employers to offer job shadowing and clinical or practicum sites, as well as volunteer, internship, and apprenticeship opportunities that help immigrant and refugee students learn about US job culture and equip them with critical workforce skills that lead to family-sustaining careers.
- Increase business leaders' awareness of the advantages of hiring skilled immigrants and refugees and point out employer barriers as well. Cultivate employer champions to increase understanding among the business community of the talents immigrants and refugees bring to the workplace and the economy.

REPLICATING AND SCALING PROMISING PRACTICES

Despite the increased interest and growth in innovative strategies to support educational and career opportunities for immigrant and refugee students, replicating and scaling new models remains a challenge. Community colleges face significant challenges in sustaining and expanding initiatives because of significant cutbacks in educational and job training funds at federal and state levels, as well as shrinking college budgets. Adult education, workforce development, and community college systems are not always well-equipped to serve immigrants and refugees at both ends of the education and skills spectrum—including those who come with prior education and experience obtained in their home countries, as well as those who are lower skilled and may lack a high school education. The ESL-contextualized model is not easy or inexpensive to implement. Sharing data across various adult education, community college, community organization, and job training systems is also challenging, as noted, and inhibits further expansion of models serving immigrants and refugees.

The Workforce Investment Opportunity Act (WIOA) of 2014, which is the federal law governing both workforce and adult education programs, provides expanded opportunities to help immigrant and ESL learners transition to postsecondary education, workforce training, and career pathways leading to employment. However, the Migration Policy Institute (MPI) has noted fundamental shortcomings in the WIOA-driven, federal–state adult education system, both in terms of scale and programming content. The current system meets less than 4 percent of the need nationally and focuses mainly on employment and postsecondary credential outcomes, while placing no value on other measures that meet ESL learners' needs in their roles as parents and citizens. Additionally, MPI notes, WIOA outcome measures do not address digital literacy skills that ensure effective integration into society.[1]

MPI's proposed English Plus Integration (EPI) model is described in the CCCIE companion volume, *Working Together: How Community Colleges and Their Partners Help Immigrants Succeed*.[2] Their chapter, excerpted from an MPI policy brief, describes how state and local adult education programs can lead efforts to scale the EPI model and partner with other key stakeholders, including employers, early childhood policymakers and organizations, local workforce development boards, and community college systems. The EPI model serves as a potential on-ramp into community college systems to help immigrant adults better understand and navigate college programs and make career pathway opportunities more accessible to all levels of English-language learners. ALLIES' Immigrant Integration Framework, which defines linguistic, social, and economic integration, and Washington State's Integrated Digital English Acceleration, which combines college, career, and life-management skills, are also described in the *Working Together* companion volume as examples of large-scale holistic frameworks that address immigrant and refugee integration along multiple dimensions.

Here are some additional approaches that community colleges and other stakeholders can consider for addressing challenges that have limited the replication of services for immigrants and refugees:

- Plan for sustainability by exploring ways to effectively leverage braided or diversified funding streams, including college funds; federal resources, such as WIOA, Perkins, Temporary Assistance for Needy Families, and the Supplemental Nutritional Assistance Program Employment and Training program, as well as other local and state funding resources.

- Other key elements of sustainability plans include using data strategically to support funding requests and strengthen advocacy initiatives; launching small-scale pilots with local philanthropic funds that may allow for greater flexibility before moving to more restrictive funding with specific outcomes required; using creative staffing approaches, including cross-training staff to allow for continuity of programming; and recruiting retired professionals as career coaches.
- Encourage peer-to-peer learning and communities of practice across community college districts and state systems to strengthen colleges' capacity to learn from one another, test new ideas, innovate, and expand educational and career training initiatives for immigrant and refugee students.

Providing immigrants and refugees pathways to higher education and workforce training enables them to achieve their educational, career, and personal goals; and, as the case studies in both volumes so vividly illustrate, our campuses, our communities, and our country benefits as well. We have shared practical models for change, recommendations for action, and resources that reflect the experiences and expertise of community colleges committed to intentionally support immigrants and refugees and raise awareness of the impact community colleges can have in their fullest social, economic, and civic integration. We encourage community college educators and the various key stakeholders with whom they partner to use this book as a way to gauge your organization's progress and take steps to initiate, strengthen, and sustain this work over time.

NOTES

1. Margie McHugh and Catrina Doxsee, *English Plus Integration: Shifting the Instructional Paradigm for Immigrant Adult Learners to Support Integration Success* (Washington, DC: Migration Policy Institute, October 2018), https://www.migrationpolicy.org/research/english-plus-integration-instructional-paradigm-immigrant-adult-learners.

2. MPI's chapter in the *Working Together* companion volume draws on research originally published by the Migration Policy Institute. MPI is an independent, nonpartisan think tank in Washington, DC, dedicated to the study of the movement of people worldwide. The full report can be found online: https://www.migrationpolicy.org/research/english-plus-integration-instructional-paradigm-immigrant-adult-learners.

About the Editors

Jill Casner-Lotto is director of the Community College Consortium for Immigrant Education (CCCIE), where she oversees research, communications, and policy development. She is the author of several CCCIE reports and articles providing best practices and resources to guide colleges in implementing immigrant and refugee education and workforce programs focused on ESL-integrated career pathways, holistic student support services, and community-based, cross-sector partnerships. Prior to her position at CCCIE, Ms. Casner-Lotto was a consultant to the Conference Board, a business research and membership organization, and vice president for policy studies at Work in America Institute, a labor-management research and membership organization. She received a BA in social sciences from Johns Hopkins University and an MA from the Medill School of Journalism at Northwestern University.

Teresita (Tere) Wisell is vice president of workforce development and community education at Westchester Community College, part of the State University of New York. She is also executive director of CCCIE. In 2014, the White House recognized Ms. Wisell as a champion of change for her contributions to workplace citizenship programs. She is a national community college Hispanic council fellow and a SUNY chancellor's award recipient. Ms. Wisell is on the board of the National Council for Workforce Education and the national advisory board of the National Skills Coalition for Skills Equity. She holds a BA in international relations and an MBA in marketing. Ms. Wisell immigrated to the United States from Cuba as a child.

About the Contributors

Juan Carlos Aguirre, after working for fifteen years in the chemical industry, joined South Texas College in 1997 as a training specialist for the Partnership for Business and Industry Training Department, where he was director from 1999 to 2002. Between 2002 and 2006, Aguirre returned to the university to get his master's degree in education, during which time he also obtained his teaching certificate and taught high school mathematics. In 2006, he returned to South Texas College as director of the Continuing and Professional Education Department. In 2013, he became associate dean of the department and in 2015 was promoted to dean of continuing professional and workforce education, serving more than 24,000 students annually in Hidalgo and Starr counties. He retired in 2019.

Walter G. Bumphus, PhD, is president and CEO of the American Association of Community Colleges. Dr. Bumphus, who has previously served in various community college leadership positions, has a bachelor's degree in speech communications and a master's degree in guidance and counseling from Murray State University, and a PhD in higher education administration from the Community College Leadership Program at the University of Texas at Austin. In 1992, Dr. Bumphus was recognized as a distinguished graduate from both Murray State University and the University of Texas at Austin. He holds the distinction of being one of the few leaders in the field of education to receive the Association of Community College Trustees Marie Y. Martin CEO of the Year Award, to chair the AACC board of directors, and to receive the AACC Leadership Award.

Montserrat Caballero is the volunteer coordinator at Pima Community College's Adult Basic Education for College and Career Division, responsible for managing all aspects of the volunteer program and student engagement programming. She has worked in adult education for three years and has tripled the number of volunteers in the division during that time. Prior to her work in adult education, she worked in the public health and nonprofit sectors.

Rolita Flores Ezeonu, EdD, has more than twenty years of experience in higher education, both in the classroom as a tenured faculty member and in administrative leadership. She has implemented and coordinated targeted initiatives and programs to strengthen student retention, transitions, and completion for students of color and immigrant and refugee populations. She was appointed vice president for instruction at Green River College in July 2018. Ezeonu served as Highline College's interim vice president for academic affairs from 2017 to 2018, and as dean of instruction for transfer and precollege education from 2008 to 2017. She earned her doctorate in educational leadership with an emphasis in the community college from Seattle University, and holds a certificate in "closing the achievement gap" from Harvard University Graduate School of Education.

Malou C. Harrison, PhD, is the president of Miami Dade College's Eduardo J. Padrón and North campuses, overseeing an enrollment of more than sixty thousand students. She is a champion for the cause of underserved students in public higher education. Harrison's passion and strategic advocacy for immigrant education and equity have propelled growing support for Deferred Action for Childhood Arrival and undocumented students on campus. Harrison serves on the Community College Consortium for Immigrant Education Blue Ribbon Panel and on the board of directors of Centro Campesino and the Miami-Dade Urban Debate League. She is a contributing author in the 2018 book, *Engaging African American Males in Community Colleges*. Her recognitions include the Jamaican Consulate General's Community Leader Award, the Nigerian American Foundation's Educational Leader Award, Florida Council for Educational Change's Leader Award, and the Florida College System's Cameron Hall Practitioner Award. A Jamaican, Harrison has four children.

Cynthia Hatch leads the English as a second language curriculum development and implementation for the American Culture and Language Institute (ACLI) at Northern Virginia Community College (NOVA). As part of the NOVA Workforce team, her focus is on creating pathways into the workforce for nonnative English speakers. Hatch received her master of arts degree in teaching English as a second language from American University, and a bachelor's degree in education from the University of Melbourne. She has taught English as a second language in various community programs in

Virginia and Maryland, including at NOVA's ACLI and Montgomery College. She also cotaught a teaching pronunciation course at American University's master of arts teaching English as a second language program. Her fields of interest include e-learning, curriculum design, and pronunciation.

Matthew Hebbard, vice president for student affairs and enrollment management at South Texas College, has served for almost sixteen years in higher education administration. He has been with South Texas College for more than thirteen years and leads the Division of Student Affairs and Enrollment Management. Hebbard is proud of his team, which provides student-centered services to ensure student success. Originally from Bloomsburg, Pennsylvania, he enjoys the community of the Rio Grande Valley with his wife, Marcela, who is from Mexico City and is a lecturer in English composition at the University of Texas Rio Grande Valley. Together, they enjoy time with their daughter, Ana, who is a rising eighth grader and proud of her bilingual and bicultural heritage.

Adam Hostetter has been an adult literacy educator for more than twenty years. He holds a degree in secondary English education from Temple University in Philadelphia. In 1995 he became a part-time, evening ESL instructor at the El Pueblo Liberty Adult Learning Center of Pima Community College's Adult Basic Education for College and Career Program in Tuscon, Arizona, the same school where he is now director. Adam has managed all aspects of the Adult Basic Education program, including oversight of programming, curriculum, professional development, volunteers, and students.

John Hunt is the executive director for adult community learning in the Division of Adult and Continuing Education at LaGuardia Community College, part of the City University of New York system, where he oversees noncredit programs in English for speakers of other languages, high school equivalency, integrated workforce development, and remedial education. With more than twenty-five years of experience in the field, he has developed contextualized English for speakers of other languages courses and services around civics and citizenship, parent engagement, and workforce development in the healthcare, retail, and hospitality sectors, including the New York City Welcome Back Center for immigrant nurses. Hunt is a member of the Community College Consortium for Immigrant Education Blue Ribbon Panel, the National Skills Coalition's Skills Equity National Advisory Panel, and the New York City Coalition for Adult Literacy Steering Committee.

Donna Kinerney, PhD, is a dean at Montgomery College in Maryland where she leads grant-funded programs providing English language, basic academic, and workforce readiness skills. She has led teams to implement federal and local grants that move learners into employment in apartment maintenance, healthcare, information technology, and most recently childcare. Kinerney testified on the Workforce Investment Act for the US House of Representatives Subcommittee on Higher Education, Lifelong Learning, and Competitiveness and is a Blue Ribbon Panel member of the Community College Consortium for Immigrant Education and the National Advisory Panel for Skills Equity for the National Skills Coalition.

Lee D. Lambert has been chancellor of Pima Community College since July 2013. Under Lambert, Pima Community College is focused on student success, connecting with business and industry to further economic development, and fostering a multicultural world that honors our differences as well as the values that unify us. He has long championed community colleges as instruments in the fight for social justice, diversity, and inclusion. Lambert has been recognized by the League of United Latin American Citizens and the Victoria Foundation for exceptional service to the Hispanic community, and by Asian Pacific Americans in Higher Education for contributions to education and to the Asian-Pacific Islander community. He received a bachelor's degree in liberal arts from Evergreen State College and a juris doctor degree from Seattle University School of Law.

Suzette Brooks Masters is a strategist, thought leader, and change maker. She maintains an active consulting practice, advising corporate, nonprofit, foundation, and government leaders on immigration and immigrant integration issues. Currently, she serves as senior strategist at Grantmakers Concerned with Immigrants and Refugees and is on the board of directors of Define American, the New York Immigration Coalition, and the Berkshire Taconic Community Foundation. From 2007 until 2016, Masters was the program director for migration at the J. M. Kaplan Fund, a private family foundation. She received a bachelor's degree in economics from Amherst College, a master's degree in economics from University of Cambridge, and a juris doctor degree from Harvard Law School.

Belinda S. Miles is president of Westchester Community College, part of the State University of New York system, which serves more than twenty-five thousand students in one of the nation's largest metropolitan areas. Her prior roles include provost and executive vice president and Eastern Campus president at Cuyahoga Community College. Dr. Miles serves on several national and regional boards of organizations focused on expanding economic and workforce development, including American Association of Community Colleges, Association of American Colleges and Universities' Presidents' Trust, Higher Education Resource Services, Westchester-Putnam Workforce

Investment Board, and Business Council of Westchester. The recipient of numerous service and leadership awards and a well-respected speaker on community college advocacy, student success, and leadership development, she holds an EdD in higher education and an master of arts in educational psychology from Columbia University Teachers College, and a bachelor of arts in political science from York College–City University of New York.

Gail O. Mellow was president of LaGuardia Community College in Long Island City, Queens, until August 2019. An expert on the history, development, and future of the American community college, she coauthored *Minding the Dream: The Process and Practice of the American Community College* and *Taking College Teaching Seriously: Pedagogy Matters!* Mellow is frequently sought as a commentator on the changing landscape of higher education, strategies for improving the nation's graduation rates, and the important role community colleges play in growing America's middle class and strengthening the economy. She received an associates degree from Jamestown Community College; a bachelor of arts from the State University of New York–Albany, where she graduated Phi Beta Kappa; and her master of arts and doctorate in social psychology from George Washington University.

Belinda S. Miles is president of the State University of New York's (SUNY) Westchester Community College, which serves more than 25,000 students in one of the nation's largest metropolitan areas. Her prior roles include system-wide provost/executive vice president and president of the Eastern Campus at Cuyahoga Community College. She is on several boards that are focused on economic and workforce development, including the American Association of Community Colleges, Block Center for Technology and Society at Carnegie Mellon, Association of American Colleges and Universities' Presidents' Trust, Hudson Valley Patterns for Progress, Westchester-Putnam Workforce Investment Board, and Business Council of Westchester. Miles is a highly regarded advocate for student success and community college leadership development, is the recipient of numerous awards, and holds an EdD in higher education and MA in education psychology from Columbia University Teachers College and a BA in political science from York College—City University of New York.

Norma Sandoval-Shinn has been an English as a second language educator for more than twenty years. Before coming to the United States, she graduated from law school and obtained a bachelor's in teaching. Her experience as an immigrant applying to graduate school and finding employment in the United States helps her understand the dreams and concerns of the students who seek her services as Pima Community College's immigrant navigator in Tucson, Arizona.

Regina Suitt is the vice president for adult basic education for college and career at Pima Community College. She has a thirty-year career in adult education. Suitt leads the largest adult education system in Arizona with multiple programs including adult basic education, adult secondary education, English as a second language, distance learning, bridge, Integrated Basic Education and Skills Training (IBEST), Transition to US Workforce, refugee education, and correctional education, as well as oversight of the largest high school equivalency testing center in Pima County. The division has received many recognitions during its forty-nine-year history with more than one hundred and fifty staff, instructors, and volunteers supporting more than six thousand students and testers each year. Regina is a member of CCCIE's Blue Ribbon Panel and the national advisory panel for skills equity for the National Skills Coalition.

Jeff Wagnitz, EdD, recently retired after eighteen years at Highline College, Washington's most diverse higher education institution. He was Highline's interim president from 2016 to 2018 and prior to that was vice president for academic affairs. Wagnitz began his thirty-seven-year career in community colleges teaching precollege and college-level English. He holds a doctorate in educational leadership from the University of Washington Tacoma. In 2016, he earned the Award of Excellence in Leadership from Washington's Community and Technical College Leadership Development Association.

Heide Spruck Wrigley, PhD, is a nationally known expert in adult second-language acquisition and immigrant education. She is the lead author of the online suite *Preparing Adult English Learners for Work and Career Pathways* funded by the Office of Career, Technical, and Adult Education and the lead author of *The Language of Opportunity: Expanding the Employment Prospects for Adults with Limited English Skills* funded by the Center for Law and Social Policy. Wrigley provides technical assistance and professional development to a range of programs serving immigrants and refugees. She is a long-term consultant for *English Innovations*, a blended learning model originally funded by the Bill and Melinda Gates Foundation and administered by OneAmerica in Seattle. She assisted in the design of *English under the Arches*, a national workplace English as a second language program created by McDonald's. Wrigley is a member of the Community College Consortium for Immigrant Education Blue Ribbon Panel and a nonresident fellow with the Migration Policy Institute. She lives in Mesilla, New Mexico.